WAR CAKE

A WITNESS IN THE SIEGE OF SARAJEVO

Linda Flynn Beekman

Published by Linda Flynn Beekman
P.O. Box 17202
Clearwater, Florida 33762

Printed in the United States of America

First Edition

ISBN 0-9755128-0-3

Library of Congress Control Number: 2004093972

Editor: Vicki Krueger

Cover Photograph copyright © Randy Allbritton/ Photodisc/
PictureQuest

Cover design by Lejla Fazlić-Omerović
Text design by Lejla Fazlić-Omerović

Back Cover Photograph: Jerry Bilton

10 9 8 7 6 5 4 3 2 1

To my son, Matthew.

To the people of Sarajevo, wherever you may be.

To Gabriele Moreno Locatelli, fellow peace activist killed in Sarajevo, October 3, 1993.

"There is a spirit which I feel that delights to do no evil ... "

—*James Naylor, English Quaker, died 1660.*

~ PREFACE ~

In 1992, the images of well-dressed civilians sprinting across intersections in Sarajevo to avoid sniper fire, and the wounded or dead lying on the streets there dominated the media and caught my attention. Little did I know in the following year, 1993, I would spend two months in Sarajevo and in the coming five years return nine more times. I went as a peace witness—an ordinary person moved to live in solidarity with civilians suffering under the siege. I was not sure how I could help, but I was certain an inner voice called me to go. My efforts to help Sarajevo grew into a project called *The Sarajevo Project*, which was eventually adopted by the St. Petersburg Friends (Quaker) Meeting.

The first indication war might come to Sarajevo was on March 3, 1992, when masked gunmen, Serb nationalists, blockaded part of the city. Sarajevans poured out into the streets, standing up to the gunmen, who by the end of the day backed down and removed the barricades. Bosnia had recently voted on a referendum, declaring its independence from Yugoslavia and ethnic Serbs had boycotted the vote.

On April 6, the gunmen returned and again partitioned the city. Thousands of Sarajevans of all ethnic and religious backgrounds gathered near the Parliament, to demonstrate for peace and unity. This time the gunmen did not back down. They shot into the crowd, killing twenty-one-year-old Suada Dilberović, a medical student from Dubrovnik. Sarajevans soon realized nationalistic Bosnian Serbs, with the support of Serbs from Serbia, had quietly dug in heavy weapons on the mountains surrounding Sarajevo, cutting the city off from the rest of Bosnia and the world. The Serbs had control of the weapons from what had been Yugoslavia, which boasted the fourth-largest army in Europe. Bosnia had police, but no army, much less army uniforms. Faced with the first winter in the war, they sewed uniforms from wool blankets.

Bosnians hold Bosnian Serb leader Radovan Karadzić (since indicted as a war criminal, but not captured) responsible for masterminding and inflicting three and a half years of terror and assault on

Sarajevo. Karadzić, originally from Montenegro, came to Sarajevo as a student and eventually became a psychiatrist there. He is charged with crimes against humanity. During the siege, more than 10,615 Sarajevans, including 1,061 children, died from snipers' bullets or exploding shells. By the end of the war, 200,000 Bosnians were dead and two million displaced or refugees.

War Cake documents the daily life of the people I met in Sarajevo during this madness, and my efforts to help them. For most people living under the siege, the concerns were the same: shelter, food, water, electricity, and the return of peace. I discovered war often brings an exhilarating rush of adrenaline, but for the most part, it is grueling and tedious: 300,000 people endured forty-three months of hunger, thirst, cold, and uncertainty.

Sarajevans caught in the siege were victims. In the initial shock of the madness, they could not believe war had come to their former Olympic City—host to the Winter Olympics in 1984. They were certain the international community, especially their neighbors in other parts of Europe, would intervene to save them. But when help did not arrive, they refused to behave as victims. During the siege, their determination to survive by maintaining the routine of their daily lives became their shield against the enemy.

In spite of daily sniper and mortar fire Sarajevans got out of bed, dressed, visited friends, and went to work, although they received no salary. Without running water, electricity, or telephone, they fell in love, got married, had babies, and educated their children. Without the promise of a tomorrow, they played the piano, danced ballet, created sculpture from broken glass, published a daily newspaper, and produced plays. Without medications or medical supplies they cared for the sick and wounded. Finally, risking their own lives, they mourned and buried their dead—when possible, in the cemeteries that dot the hills and the valley of Sarajevo, but sometimes, because of sniper fire or heavy shelling, in the yard closest to their back door.

These daring and defiant people, who resisted the guns that surrounded and molested Sarajevo, taught me to live in the present. Their resolve, persistence, and boldness in resisting the enemy inspired me to forget the limited and helpless person I thought I was.

My intention in writing this book is to document the crime of the siege of Sarajevo and to testify that ordinary people there, through the routine of their daily lives, rose above horrendous circumstances not only to survive, but to also retain their dignity and humanity.

(I have changed some names and places at the request of some of the people whose experiences are documented in this book.)

~ ACKNOWLEDGEMENTS ~

I am indebted to Bob Andelman for encouraging me to begin and to persevere in writing this book. A special thanks to Suzie Wicks for helping me get started; to Vicki Krueger for editing, and to Mimi Andelman, Kristen Hubbard and Rifat Uzunović for editing support. I am forever grateful to Lejla Fazlić-Omerović, who after finding my *War Cake* Web site by chance, volunteered to design the book, including the cover. Also, thanks to Jerry Bilton, Eleanor Caldwell, Anna Cataldi, Eva Del Cid, Susan Ey, Herb Haigh, Marlin Eric McAfee, D. Thomas Porter, John R. Smucker III, Smriti Vohra, and Linda Woodcock for reading various drafts and giving me feedback. Special thanks to Michael DeToro and Francesca Sola, my son Matthew, and my sisters Nancy Lopatin and Janis Mockler for support. Also thanks to Edward Attia for keeping my computer running. I am appreciative of my Bosnian friends, especially Farida Musanović and Gordana Simić, who patiently helped me over the past five years. And, many thanks to all those who supported my trip to Sarajevo in 1999, to work on the book.

~ CONTENTS ~

~ Chapter One ~
The Journey

As I hug and kiss my only child goodbye, my fourteen-year-old son, Matthew, at Tampa International Airport, I don't realize this is the first of many goodbyes we will say in the next five years. It is June 22, 1993, and I am on my way to Italy to join an international peace group headed for Sarajevo.

In early April 1992, nationalist Bosnian Serbs supported by Serbian leadership from Belgrade and Serb soldiers of the Yugoslav National Army dug tanks and weapons into the mountains circling Sarajevo and began firing into the city in an attempt to destroy its tradition of diversity.

Since that April, pictures of men and women of Sarajevo dressed in business clothes, sprinting across downtown intersections in an attempt to avoid sniper fire have filled the morning papers and the nightly television news programs. The scenes of dead and wounded civilians, children included, scattered on the streets of Sarajevo have haunted me. A young mother of two, interviewed on National Public Radio in Sarajevo, moved me to realize how much we had in common. She said before the war she and her husband both worked, had two cars, two kids, an apartment, a weekend cottage. A normal life.

I remember Sarajevo from the television coverage of the 1984 Winter Olympics: a snow-covered valley and mountain slopes dotted with lights sparkling like tiny diamonds. In the tradition of Bosnian hospitality, Sarajevo's residents accommodated Olympic visitors in their homes because there were not enough commercial accommodations. Now seeing civilians targeted daily and hearing rumors of concentration camps in this European country, my heart sinks. After Hitler's reign of terror in World War II, the international community vowed never again; now history is repeating itself. If genocide is happening in Bosnia, it can happen anywhere. We all are at risk.

During this time, my thoughts returned to my childhood friend Doris, who was Jewish and my best friend in the sixth grade. Although I am not Jewish, I often joined her on Saturday mornings for the children's service at her synagogue. Nazis killed many of her relatives in Germany during the Holocaust. As a child, I promised myself if it ever happened again, I'd "do something." Now I feel a responsibility to be an example for my son, to teach him by my actions, to stand against discrimination and injustice. In the early weeks of 1993, I decide to do whatever it takes to go to the former Yugoslavia and help in whatever way I am able.

Now five months after making that decision I board a plane to New York, connecting to an overnight flight to Rome. At the airport in Rome I join Anne Montgomery, a New York-based Roman Catholic nun and peace activist, who is also joining the peace initiative in Sarajevo. Anne has spent many of her sixty-six years as an advocate for peace and justice, even doing prison time for participating in anti-war demonstrations.

I have just turned fifty and am divorced. I often attend the St. Petersburg Friends (Quaker) Meeting and consider myself a pacifist. I do not have a profession or a career. I began my adult life as a ballet/jazz dancer in New York City. For many years since returning to Florida, I have earned a living cleaning houses. I have no college degree, do not know how to use a computer, and have no confidence in my writing skills. I know little about Bosnia. But I do know an inner voice compels me to go there.

Several months ago, I learned an Italian peace organization; Beati i Costruttori di Pace (Blessed are the Peacemakers) is organizing a project called We Share One Peace to establish peace camps this summer in and around Sarajevo. Soon, Beati will join with other international groups in forming the international civilian peace initiative Mir Sada! (Peace Now!). Throughout this summer of 1993, delegations of sixty to eighty people from around the world plan to stay one or two weeks in or around Sarajevo to offer moral support, urge a non-violent solution to the conflict, and seek the restoration of full human rights to all citizens. The Beati organization believes according to International Law of Human Rights, the search for peace is not an exclusive function of governments but is the right and responsibility of all people. More than 2,000 civilians from all over the world will soon arrive in Split, Croatia, to prepare to descend on Sarajevo during the first week in August, in an attempt to halt the fighting—at least for a few days. Anne and I have volunteered to spend the summer in Sarajevo as part of the organizing team.

In the days before our departure from the United States, the war in Bosnia escalated. The Serbs on the mountains circling Sarajevo hold the city in a stranglehold. No one can get in or out except on U.N. planes—if the airport in Sarajevo is even open.

When we arrive in Rome, Anne and I call the Beati headquarters in Padova, the city of St. Anthony, located about 35 minutes by train from Venice. The news is disturbing: Intense fighting continues to block all roads to Sarajevo. We are to go to Padova to wait until transportation is possible.

Late that afternoon our train pulls into Padova. The first thing I notice as we arrive at our host's apartment is the adjacent cornfield. Deep green and knee high, I come to measure my time in Padova by the growth of the cornstalks. My biggest fear is I will still be here when the corn is harvested—that I will never get to Sarajevo.

As the days get longer and the corn grows taller, Beati organizers continue to struggle with the logistical problem of getting the organizing team into Sarajevo. My determination to get to Sarajevo grows with the corn. Every breath becomes an affirmation: "I am willing and able to go to Sarajevo! I am strong and able to do what I need to do to get to Sarajevo. I am going to Sarajevo soon!" I can think of nothing else.

One day someone says to me, "What's your hurry? Enjoy where you are; you may not have it much longer." This stops me in my tracks. I begin to focus on the present, a lesson I will continue to practice in Sarajevo. (This outlook brings me inner peace on many occasions in the coming years as I wait days at a time in Ancona, Italy, for space on the airlift or for the airport to open in Sarajevo so the airlift can operate.)

Just as it looks as though Beati might abandon the whole project due to lack of entry into the war zone, someone suggests we all apply for U.N. press cards. The team consists of Anne and me—the only Americans—a young man from Spain, and a number of Italians. Immediately Anne and I contact friends in the media back home to ask whether we can represent them as correspondents in Bosnia. With media credentials, we will then apply to the U.N. press office in Split, Croatia, for a U.N. Protection Force International press card. The United Nations permits journalists to fly on planes transporting humanitarian aid from Ancona to Sarajevo; planes also fly from Split.

I contact friends at WMNF, a non-profit, listener-sponsored FM radio station in Tampa, Florida. Immediately, staff members confirm they will fax the required letter to the U.N. press office in Split. The next day, Anne receives a "yes" from a magazine in New York. Because many legitimate Italian journalists are already working in Bosnia, the Italians in our group have a more difficult time finding media representation. It will be more than a week before they begin their journey, trickling in one and two at a time. Days earlier, Anne and I agree we are willing to go to Sarajevo without the other members of the group if we are the first to receive press cards.

The reality of our departure becomes more concrete when Beati staff members take us to a warehouse containing food donated for the peace project. We painstakingly choose items we feel will sustain us in the days and weeks ahead—until the contents of the warehouse can be transported into Sarajevo along with the 2,000 people who will participate in the peace camps.

That night, we scramble to pack and repack, ditching clothes to make space for cheese, bread, dried fruit and nuts, canned tuna, chocolate, instant cereal, and soup mix. Bosnian Serbs have held the city hostage for fifteen months, cutting off the water, electricity, gas, and phone lines. Mail service, garbage pick-up, public transportation, and a consistent food supply no longer exist. At this point, I am naïve. I have no idea what it means to walk several miles to fetch a few liters of water. I am unaware of how heavy water is when carried such a distance, and I have never known how it feels to be hungry day after day.

On the morning of July 12, 1993, we stuff the last piece of cheese and bread into our luggage and board the train to Ancona. That night we cross the Adriatic Sea by ferry. We dock in Split early in the morning and grab a taxi, hurrying off to the U.N. press office, located on the second floor of the Split airport.

I hold my breath as the press officer searches his folder for the fax from my radio station. He finds it and begins to type my name and information on a blank press card. I hand him two passport-size pictures. He pastes one on the card and places the other in my file. Then he signs the card and hands it to me to sign. My heart is pounding. I'm an impostor, a feeling I will never overcome within the international community in Bosnia. Posing as a journalist intimidates me. My confidence in my ability to write is so poor, I freeze even when asked to write a short note.

On my first day in war, a young woman says to me, "Sometimes people find themselves when deprived of the familiar." She was right. Living in war forces me to confront my fear of dying—and living. In fulfilling my commitment as a witness in Bosnia, I also confront my fear of writing. (Two years later, the *Tampa Tribune* in Florida actually pays me for an article, and eight years later I graduate from college.)

But now, this unsuspecting U.N. official feeds my press card into a laminating machine. Intimidated or not, I am now officially a journalist, at least in the former Yugoslavia. I begin to breathe again and am ecstatic. My chances of getting into the besieged city of Sarajevo have just increased about 100 percent.

Three hours later, wearing our press cards clipped to our flimsy borrowed flak jackets (U.N. regulations require all passengers flying the airlift to wear bulletproof vests), Anne and I wrestle our luggage across the hot tarmac. All passengers are responsible for handling their own luggage. We climb through the tail of the cargo plane, buckle ourselves into web seats and plug our ears with yellow sponge earplugs, compliments of the English crew. We are the only passengers. Three pallets of flour roll into the plane. Second only to July 16, 1978, the day my son was born, this is the most amazing day of my life.

As the engines roar, I stare at the pallets in front of me. I don't yet understand how much Sarajevans need this flour or how difficult it will be for them to transform it into bread without access to water, electricity, or gas.

During the thirty-five minute flight, the noise from the engines prevents Anne and me from talking. It doesn't matter. We are both lost in our own thoughts and emotions. For the sake of impressing a member of the crew sitting opposite us, I try to look nonchalant— like I have done this before, but I wear a silly, nervous grin and pinch myself several times to make sure I'm not dreaming.

It seems we are barely airborne when the crewmember gets up and puts on his flak jacket. He shouts, "We are entering Bosnian Serb-held territory!" In the many flights I eventually take on these planes, I never understand the logic of wearing the flak jacket. It seems better to sit on it. But it isn't a joke; an Italian plane was shot down early in the airlift operation. Soon, we begin our approach into Sarajevo, a city so close to civilization, yet now so removed.

The plane descends quickly, almost falling out of the sky. I later learn from a U.N. newsletter, that before the war, commercial planes approached Sarajevo slowly, flying low over the city. Now, because of the threat of Bosnian Serb gunfire, pilots fly high over the mountains and don't begin their descent until they see the runway.

The plane touches down, and then races along the runway. I stretch over my shoulder to peek through the small window behind me and see a panoramic view of war.

Bordering the airport are the ruins of what was once a subdivision of modern townhouses. Some of the fiercest fighting in the war took place on this front line. Machine-gun fire and shrapnel have pockmarked every inch of standing concrete. Remnants of burnt roofing beams silhouette the sky like large charred arms reaching up to God. Broken terra cotta tiles, shattered glass, burned furniture, and chunks of concrete litter the ground. Shreds of dingy, gray lace curtains dance like ghosts in paneless windows, moving me to consider the fate of the families who once lived there.

The plane comes to an abrupt stop, but the engines do not. The

U.N. turnaround goal for the plane is fewer than ten minutes. The openness of the runway leaves the plane and everyone on the tarmac vulnerable. Quickly the tail opens and U.N. personnel roll off the pallets of flour. It is mid-afternoon and overcast. I see no color except for blue U.N. helmets and flags. Anne and I follow the flour off the plane. In turn, we each grab the extended hand of a U.N. soldier and jump down from the tailgate. Quickly, U.N. personnel load the empty pallets from a previous delivery and board departing passengers. The tail closes and the plane takes off.

We quickly leave the tarmac and enter a maze of sandbags, chain-link fencing, barbed wire, and small portable cubicles. If I had not just arrived on a plane, I would not believe this is an airport. I have no idea where I am going, no idea Sarajevo is about to grab me and not let go for the next five years.

U.N. Press Cards and other Identity Cards

~ CHAPTER TWO ~
ARRIVAL IN SARAJEVO

Sarajevo Airport resembles a Hollywood war movie set. Large wire cylinders lined with heavy white plastic hold tons of dirt. These gigantic sandbags sit side-by-side, stacked one on top of the other to form thick walls to protect airport personnel from exploding mortars or sniper fire. Considering the magnitude of the war in Bosnia, it is abnormally quiet. In past months, the United Nations and Bosnian Serbs have volleyed for control of the airport, crucial for U.N. transport of humanitarian aid into the besieged city. At present, the United Nations seems to dominate—or at least it comforts me to think so.

As soon as we leave the tarmac, we enter a dim makeshift shelter where a U.N. soldier stops us to examine our passports and press cards. He records our names, passport numbers, and press card numbers in a log and then directs us to enter one of the many portable cubicles. Inside, another soldier issues us a transport authorization to ride the tank-taxi, the only transportation available for us, between the airport and U.N. headquarters in Sarajevo about four miles away. The dangers of war do not terrify me half as much as the soldiers possibly discovering I am not a journalist.

We wait for the tank under a partly open shelter. One wall is plywood and the other three are made from panels of wire fencing. Hanging on one panel is a hand-drawn sign: *Maybe Airlines.* Around the lettering, journalists and humanitarian aid workers have fastened stickers from the countries and organizations they represent—ABC, CBS, BBC, CNN, VOX, MSF, the Canadian flag, the Swedish flag, and many others. Above the sign is a small piece of plywood with the word *destinations* printed at the top. Below is a changeable placard presently reading *Paris.* But you can choose others: *New York, Berlin, Zagreb, Rome, Geneva, or Heaven.* I don't quite understand the significance of *Maybe Airlines,* but after flying in and out of the city a few times, I do. Sometimes planes fly, but often they don't—because of mechanical problems, the weather, or a serious threat from the Serbs. Sometimes after being checked in and escorted to the waiting room, you hear a plane land and then, while waiting patiently to be called to board, you hear it take off—without you.

But now, we are not forgotten. One of the soldiers announces that the tank is here. We pull our luggage out to the muddy parking lot filled with dirty white tanks and armored personnel carriers, all caked with various layers of mud and all flying the U.N. flag. Several yards away a tank waits with the back door open. The word *taxi* is etched in the crusted mud on the back door. Suddenly I realize wearing a skirt was a mistake. There is no graceful way I can climb into this metal monster. With all my might, I jump up to sit on the tailgate, swing my feet around, and crawl to a seat. A young soldier casually throws his gun onto the seat next to me. I want to shout, "Please don't kill me with friendly fire." Two men dressed in suits also get in.

Finally the soldier jumps in, slams the door, and locks it. We head out of the parking lot and wind down a rough narrow road through the mine-infested no-man's-land I saw from the plane. It seems as if every few yards, Serb, Bosnian, or U.N. soldiers stop us at a check-point. At one of the barricades, a guard demands to see everyone's identification. The soldier riding with us swings the back door open and we present our press cards and passports.

Three rings of power operate in Sarajevo, controlling the flow of traffic and aid in and out of the city. The strongest is Bosnian Serb, followed by the United Nations. The Bosnian government is third, but has little power except in keeping its citizens in Bosnia. A few weeks before my arrival, Bosnian Serb soldiers at one of these check-points stopped a U.N. armored personnel carrier (under French Peacekeepers escort) transporting the Bosnian Deputy Prime Minis-ter, Hakija Turajlic, from the airport into Sarajevo. The Serbs ordered him out of the tank and shot him on the spot. Although the United Nations controls the airport and airlift, its activity is subject to Serb power. The killing of Turajlic outraged Bosnians. (The inability of the U.N. Protection Force to protect those under its care continually brings criticism from Bosnians and the international community. The worst incident comes on July 13, 1995, in the U.N.-declared "safe area" of Srebrenica, when more than 7,000 Bosnian Muslim men and boys are taken and executed by Bosnian Serbs, under the command of General Ratko Mladić, while Dutch peacekeepers stand by, helpless. The Dutch commander's call for air strikes is rejected.)

Soon our tank-taxi rolls onto what is left of the narrow residential streets of Dobrinja, a small suburb between the airport and Sarajevo. Dobrinja has endured its own siege. The war's front line winds through the area and has caused residents to suffer from some of the fiercest fighting. A Serbian sniper positioned in the steeple of the Serbian Church has killed or wounded many civilians. If mortars haven't torn up the streets by now, the tanks do. Some of the high-rise apartment buildings were newly built when the Serbs started shelling in April 1992, but now there isn't a building standing without major damage—roofs, outer walls and windows missing. Heavy mortar and sniper fire have forced residents to bury their dead in makeshift graves only a few feet from apartment buildings. Dobrinja is very open with few places to hide. To shield themselves from shelling and the sniper fire, civilians move about in a maze of deep trenches they dug and narrow paths lined high with sandbags.

As our tank rocks along, I feel claustrophobic and cramped. The thought of being trapped in a fire in this tin can terrifies me. Soon we turn into the razor wire-fortified complex of the former telephone communications building, the PTT, now U.N. headquarters in Sarajevo. We have officially arrived.

As the tank dumps us in the middle of the empty parking lot, it starts to drizzle. We cannot enter the PPT building because it is mid-afternoon and after-hours for journalists, so we take shelter under the overhang. I feel numb and lost.

My hand clutches a piece of paper with the address of a cafe, now functioning as an office for a Frenchman, John Paul, who is a friend of Beati organizers in Padova. If we can find the place and his secretary, she will give us shelter. There is no public transportation. A few taxis operate, but at the black market rate of fifty dollars and up. I feel like a refugee. Before I left the States, and while I was in Padova, I attempted to prepare myself for this experience, but now I realize it is impossible to foresee the challenges of war. All I can do now is engage each moment as it comes.

Gunfire echoes in the distance and is closer and more frequent than I expected. Within a few days, I come to accept the sound as part of the background noise, but I always attempt to calculate the distance between the sound and me.

Several people come and go from the PTT building, but Anne and I seem frozen—unable to figure out what it is we need to do. Then, a pickup truck with the United Nations High Commissioner for Refugees insignia on its doors comes through the gate. A young man and woman wearing heavy flak jackets jump out and rush into the building. They quickly reappear and ask if we need a ride. I show them the address on the crumpled paper and they say, "Jump in, the cafe is next door to our office." I feel overjoyed and relieved. We throw our luggage in the back of their truck, and the four of us squeeze into the cab and race down the main street, "Sniper Alley," at eighty miles an hour. I don't know their country of origin, but like most internationals (and many Bosnians) I will meet, they speak fluent English. They work for Solidarity, a humanitarian organization.

This is the first of many rides I will hitch between the PTT building/U.N. headquarters and downtown Sarajevo. Like Blanche Du-Bois in *A Streetcar Named Desire*, I will, on numerous occasions in Bosnia, "depend on the kindness of strangers."

It is summer and I know there is green, but I see only gray. A blanket of soot and chalky dust coats everything. The city has been under attack for well over a year—long enough for trees to take root in collapsed buildings. Tons of rotting garbage piled on the street and overflowing from large metal bins burns and smolders, polluting the air. Rusty trams and overturned cars gutted by fire stand throughout the city as mini-monuments, marking places where unexpected violence brazenly interrupted the pulse of daily life.

It is difficult for me to imagine what the city looked like before Serb shelling reduced it to rubble. In my many visits to Sarajevo, residents tell me how beautiful their city was before the war, but it will be years before I see the Sarajevo they remember.

In addition to snipers' bullets and artillery shells, pedestrians battle potholes, twisted metal, broken glass, and unpredictable traffic. Gas is scarce and expensive, and vehicles few, but beware of those that are on the road. There is no electricity to light traffic signals or a single police officer willing to stand in full view of snipers to direct traffic. Speeding is the norm, along with driving on the sidewalk or down the wrong side of the street. In case of an accident, there is no one to call, much less anyone to sue.

We arrive at our destination, a five-story building that is home to several humanitarian organizations and U.N. troops. Next door, across a small brick plaza we find the cafe, and Jana, the secretary, who will take us to her apartment. She is Serb—Orthodox. During the siege, Muslims, Catholics, Orthodox, and Jews live together as they did before the war. Many Bosnian Serbs did leave Sarajevo to join nationalistic Serbs attacking Sarajevo and the rest of Bosnia, but many stayed and even served in the Bosnian army. To avoid offending the Serbs among them, especially family members in mixed marriages, Sarajevans never refer to the Serbs attacking Sarajevo as *Serbs*, but always as the *aggressor* or *crazy people*, or *bearded monsters*, or *Chetnik*—the name of nationalistic Serbs who, in World War II, killed thousands of Bosnian Muslims.

Jana has been waiting for us for several hours. By now, it's after three in the afternoon and she is ready to go home. She says everyone feels more secure if they are home by early afternoon. Immediately we load our things into her friend's car and head halfway back in the direction of the PTT building, but not via sniper alley. The driver chooses an alternate, slower route winding through narrow streets behind tall apartment buildings. Throughout the siege, cars and pedestrians travel this route to get from one end of the city to the other. Later in the summer, I walk the route several times.

In addition to depending on strangers for their kindnesses, I also count on their sound judgment and honesty. In the next five years, I log 100,000 commercial air miles between the United States and

Italy and fly U.N. cargo planes more than a dozen times between Sarajevo and Zagreb, Ancona, or Split. After the Dayton Peace Agreement in November 1995, when the roads into the city open, I beg
rides on convoys from Split to Tuzla, and Split to Sarajevo and from
Tuzla to Sarajevo. During these journeys, I put my life in the hands
of strangers who never disappoint me. Quite the opposite: poor,
hungry, and tired people house me, share their food, make me coffee, give me directions, and help me carry my luggage. Even later this
summer I arrive at the PTT building after traveling to Italy to buy
supplies. Unable to hitch a ride, I walk toward the center of town,
pulling my suitcase filled with food for those in our neighborhood.
No one ever does more than stare longingly at the bags.

Now, I unquestioningly depend on our host Jana and her friends.
As we approach her apartment building, she tells us the bad news—
not only does part of her apartment, including our room, face Sniper
Alley; it is on the ninth floor. Without electricity, there is no elevator. I thought I had mentally prepared myself for all the hardships I
might encounter in a war zone, but I never considered climbing nine
flights of stairs. The only thing worse than climbing up is going back
down to get the rest of the luggage.

Jana shows us our room and nervously explains that, although
she nurtures a small rooftop garden, she doesn't have enough food
to feed us. We assure her we understand and have brought enough
supplies to be self-sufficient. Actually, she is the self-sufficient one.
She doesn't say it in words, but I sense her kitchen is off-limits to us.
Her survival depends on careful conservation, storage, and recycling
of supplies. It is the first time I read by a small lamp made from a tin
can and tuna oil.

As we unpack, Anne admonishes me for giving our host a good
part of our food supply—especially the large hunk of Parmesan
cheese. I anticipate we will stay with her longer than we actually do
and I am anxious to assure Jana we won't be a burden. Two days later
when we decide to relocate, I understand Anne's concern because
our remaining food supply will probably not last more than two
weeks. I have never been forced to ration food and do not know

exactly how much we need to sustain us. Even attempting to figure it out makes me hungry.

Living in a vulnerable ninth-floor apartment is not our only surprise. Jana shares her home with a German shepherd and a cat. Maintaining pets during a war shocks me—especially the monster dog that races from room to room chasing the cat, which likes to take shelter in our room. I carefully hide our food, remembering a visit to my mother's cousin in Paris. Her dog ate a whole box of expensive French chocolates I had placed in my open suitcase. Now, food is a matter of survival.

Jana says her pets comfort her and the neighbors, reminding them of normal times. Even during the most difficult periods, her neighbors save small scraps of food for the animals, which by necessity have become vegetarians. She said many nights during heavy shelling she and the dog cower in the bathroom, the only room without windows. On my first trip up to her apartment, I couldn't help but notice the gaping hole in the outside wall between the eighth and ninth floors, where a mortar shell barely missed her apartment.

It is almost dark as Anne and I finish unpacking. Exhausted by our journey from the press office in Split to Sniper Alley in Sarajevo, we pull out the sleeper sofa and crawl into bed. As the day fades and darkness takes the room, I feel too tired to sleep.

Suddenly, explosions not far off bring us to a sitting position. The room is bright with dots of light sparkling on the ceiling and walls, reminding me of the tiny specks of light reflected from a glass ball hanging above a ballroom floor. The light is from outside, filtering in through small holes in the outer window shutter. In a city without electricity, I wonder where the light is coming from. I jump up and peek through the cracks. Tracer shells followed by tails of gray and white smoke crisscross in the sky, painting it red. A large building burns at the other end of town. The entire sky looks like a Turner painting of the War of 1812; I am terrified.

Like two small children having a nightmare, Anne and I run to find Jana in the kitchen, talking with a neighbor. She says this is nothing compared to what they have experienced in the past year.

She doesn't seem concerned, so Anne and I return to our bed. But I am shaken. What have I done coming to Sarajevo? Am I crazy? In a single day, war has sucked me into its reality, obliterating my memories of home and demanding my soul. As the light in the room begins to fade, I scribble in my journal: "I don't want to die. I want to see Matthew again, but I must be here. I give myself over to the spirit that moves me. I will live my mission. I will confront my fear of dying. I come here because if Matthew or I were in the same situation I would want someone to come for us. I am strong, alert. I will listen, pay attention and transform my fear." I have chosen to be in this war in Sarajevo. There is nothing left to do but live my decision.

Left: Linda Beekman Right: Edith Daly
Photo: Edith Daly

Dobrinja
Photo: Linda Beekman

~ CHAPTER THREE ~
ORIENTATION TO WAR

Disjointed, sharp, intense, and unpredictable. Life in Sarajevo resembles shrapnel. The shell explodes and thousands of razor-edged fragments shatter and fly in every direction. As a friend here says, "Each piece is marked with its own destiny." Some etch the sides of buildings or fall to litter the street. Others cut into flesh, sometimes superficially, but, more often, severely wounding or killing. One determined fragment shattered the window of a friend's apartment, traveled through two inner walls to the kitchen, finally denting the refrigerator at the exact place she had been standing moments earlier.

In this disjointed existence, the common thread of *need* connects everyone. For all, the struggle is the same: Find enough water, food, fuel, and shelter to survive another day.

It's 5 a.m. on my first full day in Sarajevo and I awake to a clicking and grinding noise on the street below. I hear our host, Jana, rush down the stairs. Her trip back up the stairs is not so fast. Then, from the bathroom, I hear water flowing into the large plastic storage barrel. Water has arrived. Last night she told us that she and her neighbors have negotiated with a person with a large dolly to cart water to the building. Reluctantly, Anne and I jump out of bed to help. How can we expect her to lug water up the stairs for us? Back home, I thought I considered the hardships of war. Hauling water up nine flights of stairs wasn't one of them.

I soon learn hauling water is at the heart of activity in Sarajevo— the pulse of the city. Early in the siege, the aggressor deliberately destroyed the main pumping station and shut off the others. Few sites provide water. Often individuals walk several miles through sniper fire and then stand in line for hours to fill their plastic jugs, gallon canisters, and plastic Coke and Pepsi bottles. They cart them home on anything with wheels: baby buggies, strollers, little red wagons, skateboards, sleds with roller skates attached, bicycles, trolleys, and dollies. Those without wheels drape a leather belt over their shoulders and attach a canister to each end. Stooped with their heavy load, these souls remind me of beasts of burden plowing a field.

The most popular and reliable source of water is the brewery near the Miljacka River and the old, now burned, city library. Built in 1881, the basement of the brewery accesses natural spring water used for making beer. The queues for water are always long and, at times, the target of Serb shells. Often the water pressure is low. One woman tells me she and family members once took turns spelling each other in line for twenty-eight hours, all for only a few liters of water. The brewery also provides water for fire trucks. A favorite shortcut to the building is a footbridge twenty feet above the shallow river. Aggressor shelling has left the bridge with one narrow girder, wide enough to accommodate one foot at a time. I use the bridge most of the summer until the day it occurs to me that if a sniper shoots me while crossing, the fall will double my chances of getting hurt.

Residents also use water from the river, gather rainwater, and catch the evening dew on awnings built of plastic supplied by the United Nations High Commissioner for Refugees. The awnings angle down and inward, draining the dew down into window boxes and tin-can gardens growing in almost every window. The UNHCR plastic is a valuable commodity, used for everything from covering broken windows or damaged roofs, to wrapping cookies for a child's party.

With a turn of a valve and the flip of a switch, and with massive shelling, the enemy has reduced this city to primitive life—not bad in itself if that is a culture's reality, but this was not so in Sarajevo. Sarajevans hate being thought of as primitive, because long ago residents adopted modern customs. The city boasts one of the earliest aqueduct systems in Europe. Before the siege, Sarajevo enjoyed a fine library containing centuries-old books, a modern hospital, a university with medical and dental schools, music and art academies, a ballet company, a symphony orchestra, a national theater, an opera company, and an international airport, and in 1984, Sarajevo hosted the Winter Olympics. Sarajevans consider their city to be as cosmopolitan and contemporary as any other city in Europe. As the international community permits the siege to lag on, Sarajevans bitterly remind the world they are a part of Europe, and ask, "Would you allow this to happen to Paris or Rome?"

At 9 a.m. John Paul, Jana's boss, arrives with his car and takes Jana and us to the office where we met her yesterday. Anne and I first met John Paul on the ferry from Ancona to Split. We saw him again the next morning at the airport in Split, where he flew into Sarajevo on an earlier plane. The Beati organizers in Padova told us to look for him, as he was their friend and could probably arrange for us to stay with Jana. I am not sure what his business is here, and his aloof and impatient attitude leaves me afraid to ask.

When we arrive at the office, we find two university students who volunteer to take us on a walking tour of the city. Like all young adults I meet during the war, Olga and Senada wait impatiently for peace so they can get on with their lives. Another young woman I later meet says, "I am waiting to catch my train, but I am afraid it is going to pass me by."

Before we begin our tour, Olga and Senada remind Anne and me to be aware: "If you can see the mountain, they can see you! Pay attention to what people are doing and do the same. If they run across an intersection, run!"

We ignorantly ask, "Where are the safe places?" Patiently they tell us, "There are none. Shells don't discriminate. They fall from the sky without notice. It doesn't matter if you are Muslim, Serb, Croat, Jew, or even American."

As we leave the building, I notice a number of men and women digging in the treeless park across the street. Olga explains, "The first winter of the siege caught us off guard because we didn't think the attack would last so long. People were desperate for fuel, so they cut down the trees in this park. Now, we face our second winter, so they are digging out the roots to burn for fuel."

Before the war, wood-burning stoves and ovens were not widely used in Sarajevo, but now, tinsmiths, artisans common in Sarajevo, fashion small tin stoves capable of burning wood or adapting to gas if it is available. Most include a tiny oven. Many people have installed these tin lifesavers in their living rooms or in whatever room is most suitable for winter hibernation. An ugly exhaust pipe protrudes through a window or outer wall, channeling the smoke outside, polluting the air, and blackening the outside of the building.

To avoid wasting energy, women share ovens in warm weather. Neighbors bring enough wood, paper, or even old shoes to fuel the fire for their bread, or pita, a dough normally filled with meat or vegetables, but in wartime often eaten empty, or sometimes filled with a tangy paste made from powered yeast.

As we walk on, I notice the words *pazi snajper* (beware of sniper) scribbled on buildings and lampposts, especially at intersections. The word *skloniste* (shelter) identifies buildings with basements where people can take refuge during shelling. To shield themselves from being shot while walking on main streets and intersections facing the mountain, pedestrians weave around buildings, slabs of concrete, and stacks of shipping containers.

The words *Pink Floyd* decorate one gigantic slab of concrete shielding a small intersection near the center of town. In a few weeks, someone will paint over it a picture of a boy with wings and the words, *SKID ROW I'll remember you Sebastian!*

One evening later in the summer, I visit a friend near that intersection. After leaving her apartment, a dog growls and barks at me. Frightened and disoriented, I turn left instead of right and find myself on the wrong side of that slab—in front of it, instead of behind it. Terrified, I freeze, not knowing where to turn. I am lucky it is night.

Now, as we move down the street, I hear loud noises coming from a destroyed building. Olga says, "People are gathering fuel, stripping uninhabitable buildings of wood or anything else that will burn. Snow comes early. We are constantly scavenging. By now, we realize no one is going to rescue us. We must save ourselves."

We turn onto the main street and Olga and Senada frequently stop to say hello and introduce us to their friends. In this city of 300,000 (600,000 before the war) it seems everybody knows everybody. Without phone or mail service, Sarajevans hunger for news and communication. There is never a lack of topics to discuss: the dead, the wounded, disappointment in the lack of air strikes, and the amount of humanitarian aid received, or not received. Women exchange war recipes, some inherited from their mothers from World War II, and some just created.

A few days later, when I venture out on the street solo for the first time, I meet some of these people again. They greet me as though we are old friends. In these early days, I fall in love with Sarajevo and its people. Except for the danger of sniper fire and shelling, it's easy to manage as a pedestrian. I feel comfortable in the city—as though I have been here my whole life. By focusing intensely on the present, the past and future have melted away. I write in my journal, "Today I feel hungry all day and can hear sniper fire everywhere, but it is good to be here. I am willing and able to be here. I open myself to what is here, to the people, their pain, hunger and thirst."

War heightens my senses, especially smell. As we continue our walk, my clothes and hair quickly absorb the stench of smoldering garbage. No gasoline, so no garbage pick-up! Olga and Senada are apologetic about the condition of their city. They assure us before the aggressor attacked, Sarajevo didn't look or smell like the slum it has become. Senada says, "We have many fine shops, restaurants and outdoor cafes, but now nothing is open. You must come back when this war is over."

In the early afternoon, Senada leads us up stairs cut into the side of a hill, and then on to a road running through a massive tunnel. After a short walk, we exit out the other side. A few more blocks and we arrive at her apartment, where she lives with her parents. From the living room window, she points to a building in the distance and says, "It is my grandmother's house, but the aggressor controls her neighborhood. I have not seen or spoken with her since the war started."

Senada's parents are frightfully thin. Her mother, who was overweight when the war started, jokes about always wanting to look like a model, but quickly turns her attention toward us. She eagerly asks us two questions everyone we meet will sooner or later ask. "Why did you come to this hell?" and "How long are you staying?" The second question is all-important. If anyone risks staying here more than two weeks, it is interpreted as a sincere concern for Sarajevo; they can be trusted. Sarajevans resent those who come for a few days and never leave the Holiday Inn (home to many journalists) and are never without their flak jackets. We tell them we are staying for at least two months.

To live in solidarity with civilians, no one in our Beati group will wear flak jackets, except when the U.N. regulations require it during transportation in U.N. vehicles. Bulletproof vests don't always protect anyway. (Several years later when I visit the city of Tuzla, a Bosnian woman who worked for the United Nations at the airport told me one day when the Serbs shelled the airport, a U.N. soldier asked her why she wasn't wearing her flak jacket. Sarcastically, she said, "The United Nations did not issue me one. I am only Bosnian. My life is not worth as much as yours." A week later Serbs again shelled the airport, killing that same soldier, who was wearing his flak jacket.)

As to why I came to Sarajevo, I explain to Senada's parents that their suffering moved me. I want to help or at least show them I care. I tell them I have a son, who turns fifteen in two days. One day we might be in the same position and would want someone to help us. They say they aren't sure they would leave peace to be in war, but that our presence means a lot to them. Senada's mother says, "You and Anne are only two, but you break our feeling of isolation. You make us feel the world has not forgotten us."

In the next moment, before I realize what she is doing, Senada's mother serves us each a bowl of thin bean soup. They have so little I am ashamed to eat their food, but if I don't, I fear hurting her feelings. Senada and her family, like all civilians, depend on U.N. humanitarian aid: dried beans, flour, rice, oil, and, sometimes, powered milk and sugar. The airlift transporting the aid operates from the municipal airport in Ancona. Deliveries are erratic because often the aggressor shells the Sarajevo airport, forcing it to close.

The flour sitting in front of us yesterday on the transport plane was brought for the main bread bakery located in the neighborhood where we are staying, but the bakery needs both electricity and gas to operate. Rarely does the city have both at the same time. Many days there is no bread. I soon come to concretely appreciate the meaning of the words, "Give us this day our daily bread." On the days I have bread to eat, I am not so hungry.

Shelling has destroyed many shops; the rest are closed. Prices on the black market soar. Olga says Sarajevo is the most expensive city in the world. A jar of honey at the open-air market is fifty German marks, about thirty dollars. A large jar of Nescafe instant coffee costs 100 German marks, sixty dollars. Even if one has money, there is very little to buy. Bosnian money is almost worthless, so the German mark has become the official currency. The American dollar is also sometimes accepted. Local people tell me items such as gasoline and food are often obtained illegally from the United Nations. (Throughout the siege I continually question why the United Nations can't bring more practical aid into the city for civilians—especially after seeing U.N. personnel loading crates of beer and liquor into a tank at the PTT/U.N. headquarters.)

We say goodbye to Senada's parents and head for the last stop on our tour, the International Peace Center, a local peace organization Beati organizers hope will support the peace camps. The office is in a building next to the Presidency in the center of town. As I climb the pitch-dark stairway I cling to the handrail and make a mental note to keep my flashlight with me in the future.

We find several young adults and teenagers lounging in the office. Occasionally someone picks up a phone receiver in hopes that maybe a miracle has happened and the enemy has restored phone service. They stare longingly at their computers. Later, I learn some mornings the kitchen in the basement distributes bread spread with salty cheese—a good enough reason to hang out here.

We begin to discuss Beati's plan for peace camps in the three warring areas: Serb Ilidza, and Croat Kiseljak, both only a few miles from Sarajevo, and Muslim Sarajevo. A heavy silence falls over the room. The group firmly explains, "First, Sarajevo is not only 'Muslim,' but ethnically mixed. Second, the people of Sarajevo did not start this conflict. Nationalistic Serbs under the leadership of Radovan Karadzić attacked the city. We citizens of Sarajevo fight only to defend ourselves." The international media has billed the conflict a civil or ethnic war, but local people tell me Serbia initiated the aggression in order to grab land for a "Greater Serbia"—a long-held Serb nationalist idea. The Peace Center and other groups in Sarajevo supporting Beati's project want the camps only in Sarajevo, because the city has always been and still is committed to diversity and peace. They tell me for more than a thousand years, Bosnia has never crossed its borders to attack anyone.

Suddenly I feel totally in the dark about this conflict in Bosnia. I attempt to hide my ignorance by keeping quiet. Anne and I agree to send their objections back to Padova via short-wave radio and to meet with them again.

As we walk back to Jana's office, I am exhausted and hungry. My stomach is growling. It is already evident my body is expending more energy than I am consuming. I am also thirsty. It's July and hot. Back in the office, I find an apple in my backpack I forgot I had. As I pull it out, Jana, Olga, and Senada all stare at it as though they have never seen an apple before. Actually, they haven't seen one in months. I give it to them to share. Although I see people here have no extra body fat, I am ignorant of what it really means—of the suffering that hunger has caused during these past 15 months.

On the way home, I ask John Paul if we can take a quick detour to look for the apartment of a woman named Renata, a twenty-year-old ballet dancer whose parents now live in Florida. When the war started, they were visiting their son, who is going to school in the United States, so they couldn't return to Sarajevo. I met them by chance a few days before I left Florida. They told me they had not been able to contact Renata for many months but thought she was expecting a baby. They asked me to take fifty dollars and a small package to her. (Years later they tell me they gave me only fifty dollars because they thought I was so shy they didn't believe I would ever make it to Sarajevo.)

Now, I feel an urgency to find Renata, to deliver her parents' parcel and the money. Hopefully, I will be able to report to them she is alive and well. Her father drew me a map marking the closest landmark to their apartment, the Hotel Europa. He described the hotel as a stately Austro-Hungarian building. He didn't know that early in the siege enemy firebombs hit the building, occupied then by women and children, refugees from eastern Bosnia. Fragments of burning wood from the hotel flew across the street onto the roof of a family's top-floor apartment. While the husband struggled to keep the fire from spreading, his wife and seven-year-old son took shelter in the basement. When the boy heard the screams of the women and children in the hotel, he cried and shouted, "Why doesn't someone help those people, they are burning." When firefighters arrived, they found no water pressure in the neighborhood. As they struggled to extinguish the blaze with one tank of water, the aggressors on the hills above aimed their guns and began shooting, wounding two firefighters, but no one died there that day. When the ashes cooled the women and children returned to their home in ruins of the Hotel Europa.

Now, as we pass the hotel and turn onto Renata's narrow street, ragged children play soccer on the bare concrete of what once was the hotel lobby. Days later, I walk by the building and make the mistake of giving several children candy. Before I can blink, dozens of outstretched hands smother me. As I fill one hand, it disappears for a moment and then returns empty. The frenzy frightens me and after that, I avoid going near the building. Two years later after visiting the mother of a paraplegic child in the Hotel Central, another shelter for refugees in the same neighborhood, I realize I had nothing to fear from those refugee children—only the awareness that their needs were so great, and could not alleviate their suffering. Later in the summer, Beati organizes a shipment of food into Sarajevo and we make packages—a few kilos of flour, sugar, and dried beans for each family living in the Hotel Europa.

Now, as the car stops in front of Renata's apartment building, I feel a sense of accomplishment. I have found her, or at least her apartment. A neighbor upstairs tells us until her baby is born Renata is staying with her husband's family in Alipasino Polje, a neighborhood at the other end of town, near the PTT/U.N. headquarters. Tomorrow we will go there.

Today has been both ordinary and exceptional. We have casually walked the streets of a city where from April 1992 to December 1995, the aggressor killed 10,615 people, including 1,061 children. I catch myself wondering if I am suicidal and if this is my game of Russian roulette.

As John Paul drives us home, he says he will pick us up in the morning at nine, but we never see him again. Later that evening, he dies when his car collides with a U.N. tank on Sniper Alley near the PTT/U.N. headquarters.

Photo: Edith Daly

Water
Photo: Edith Daly

~ CHAPTER FOUR ~

RENATA

I feel a special connection to Renata the first time I hear her parents say her name—more than a month before I actually meet her. *Renata*, meaning *re-born*, is also the name of a cherished friend, Sister Renata, a Swiss Dominican I met in Boston in the late '60s. This caring nun threw me a lifeline at a time when I was emotionally drowning. Ironically, I will repay the favor with another Renata. During a chance meeting with her parents a few days before I leave Florida, I learn that their daughter is a ballet dancer. Because of my many years at the ballet barre in my youth, this connection makes me feel as though I already know her.

After learning about Renata, my journey to Sarajevo takes on a special purpose. I have come on behalf of the Beati peace project, but now I am also here for a person—an individual with a face, a name, and a family waiting back in Florida for news of whether she is alive or dead. From now until the siege ends, I devote a great part of every day to helping Renata in some way. Many nights when I am back home in Florida, she finds her way into my dreams—always she has escaped from Sarajevo.

Now, at last I am about to meet Renata. Anne and I climb the stairs to the fifth floor of a high-rise apartment building, one of many across from the PTT/U.N. headquarters. The glass in the stairwell windows is shattered. Piles of trash and dust sit undisturbed on each floor. As I knock on the apartment door, I feel a certain sense of accomplishment—at least I have found her. Quickly the door opens and a small, wiry woman with permanent-waved hair, Renata's mother-in-law, greets us in Bosnian. She is expecting us. There are no phones working, but news travels fast in Sarajevo. She calls to Renata, who immediately appears. She is twenty, but looks much younger. Deep reddish-gray shadows frame her large dark brown eyes. Traces of red run around and under her fingernails, which are bitten down to the quick. The fullness of her face cannot hide her vitamin-deficient diet. She wears her long auburn hair pulled back, in a traditional ballet style. Scared of shelling, and stressed from the war and her pregnancy, she smokes one cigarette after another. Unfortunately her husband is in the army and is paid in cigarettes.

Renata seems delicate, but I know that dance has developed her balance, flexibility, and stamina—skills necessary for her to perform this choreography of war. With balance she navigates on foot through war-littered streets from her apartment near the Bascarsija, the old part of town built in Turkish times, to this high-rise in Alipasino Polje. Carefully calculating her steps, she slowly glides across the single narrow girder remaining on the footbridge crossing the Miljacka River near her apartment. Flexibility enables her to bend both physically and mentally in order to meet the aggressor's demand for constant change, sometimes getting up at three in the morning to vacuum and clean because that's when the water or electricity is on.

Years of repetitive ballet exercises have developed her stamina. It is second nature for her to push against herself—each time stretching her leg a little higher—each time attempting one more pirouette. Stamina sustains her through forty-one months of terror.

As a young teenager, Renata spent several summers in upstate New York visiting an uncle, so she speaks English well. My firsthand news of her parents thrills her. (In the years to come, I fill the role of messenger on many occasions for people in and out of Sarajevo. Each time, I feel a privilege and solemn responsibility in being the link connecting them with their families and friends. In 1996, when I deliver money from Renata's father in Florida to his elderly mother in Tuzla, she sits glued next to me on the sofa, crying and touching my hands and face, saying, "When I touch you I feel like I am touching my son, because you have touched him.")

Now, this child/woman, eight months pregnant and two months shy of her twenty-first birthday, sits on the edge of her chair, questioning me and absorbing every detail I can remember about my chance meeting with her parents less than one month ago.

Renata's parents left Sarajevo in late 1991, to visit her brother who was attending high school in the United States. They wanted her to go with them, but she had recently started working as a professional dancer with the Sarajevo Ballet and didn't want to take time off. In March 1992, a few days before the war started, Renata, missing her family and sensing some unknown trouble coming, flew to Belgrade, then the capital of a joined Yugoslavia, to apply for a visa to visit her parents in the United States. Authorities in Belgrade denied the visa, claiming she could not leave because she was born in Serbia and still had military obligation there.

While in Belgrade, Renata visited her grandfather, who lived just outside the capital. She said, "He pleaded with me not to return to Sarajevo, but I had my job in the ballet, and I never dreamed the enemy would surround us, shoot unarmed civilians, and try to destroy the whole town.

"When I was ready to return to Sarajevo, I waited at the airport in Belgrade for several hours. There was a possibility we would not fly at all. Then finally we left on a small plane. We flew low and I could see a lot of fire and smoke on the ground. I didn't know it then, but I returned on the last commercial flight into Sarajevo. A few days later Serbs began shelling the city.

"For the first two months I didn't know what was going on, except they shelled us every day, killing a lot of people. None of us could believe what was happening. I had spent all my money on the ticket to Belgrade, so I had no money to buy food. My boyfriend's family invited me to stay with them. Soon, we decided to get married.

"During the first fifteen days of the attack, I called my parents in the States from a warehouse in the basement of his apartment building. I would break the line several times, hanging up and then calling back, so the enemy couldn't trace the call. If they did, they would shell the building. Then suddenly, the phones died because the enemy cut electricity to the city. It felt like the end of life. We couldn't talk to people outside of Bosnia. We couldn't even find out what was happening in the other parts of town.

"When telephone calls had been possible, they were routed

through Serbia, so we were careful in our conversations not to give
the enemy any information that could be used against us militarily,
or that would further degrade us morally. When I talked to my parents, I pretended everything was fine. I could not talk about the real
situation here. I could not let someone in Serbia hear me say 'Serbs
are killing me! I cannot breathe! I am sitting in a filthy basement with
rats!'

"In Sarajevo we have always had mixed marriages—almost half
and half," says Renata. "Now, the enemy doesn't care if their grenades
kill Serbs. It doesn't make sense that Serb shells kill even Serbs. They
cannot say they are fighting for Serbia or the Orthodox Church if
they kill their own people. They don't care. They are crazy people in
a position of power. If a person is religious, then they are not going
to kill. Nobody has the right to kill."

Almost a year ago, on September 19, the day before her twentieth
birthday, Renata and her sister-in-law went to a neighbor's courtyard
to drink coffee with him. Renata says, "He recycled pieces of old
grenades into new ones, so the courtyard was full of ammunition
and explosives. It was a beautiful, quiet sunny day. The birds were
singing. Our friend went upstairs to his apartment to make coffee.
Suddenly the men on the mountains begin to shell.

"Seven grenades fall around me. One explodes about a meter
from me. I am lucky because a large machine used to grind stone
shields me from the explosion. A piece of shrapnel hits my leg, but
only burns a small piece of skin. I pull the metal out. Then I realize
all the people we passed coming into the courtyard are dead. One
is without a head. Another has his insides on the outside. Some are
without arms or legs. Brains and blood are all around. I stand in the
middle of the courtyard, my face black from gunpowder, looking for
a place to hide. I keep muttering, 'I don't want to die. Please, I don't
want to die.'

"After that, I couldn't go out for forty days. It is a custom for Muslim people to stay inside for forty days after someone dies. I didn't
do it for that reason, but that's how I felt—I couldn't go out. I didn't
want to go for water. On that day in the courtyard, I sat enjoying the

sunshine with our neighbors. Then they all died. On that day, I was one step from death. My birthday came but I could not celebrate. I understood then how my life, my future, was going to be. It was not going to get better."

By late December 1992, Renata and her husband return to live in the apartment where she lived with her parents before they went to the United States. Most of the time her husband was working with the police, defending the city. On New Year's Eve, she was alone in the apartment. She says, "I knew the aggressor would shell the city on New Year's Eve. At twelve o'clock, instead of fireworks, they start shooting—killing people. I sat the whole night on the floor in my hall bathroom, the only room without windows. Without electricity, I sat in the dark talking to myself, 'Why am I here, sitting in my bathroom?' All the time I think, 'Where is God? There is no God. If he is here somewhere, then he will find me here sitting alone in the dark, in my bathroom, scared, waiting for someone to kill me.' Before the war, I had everything I needed in my life. I was happy. I know there is nothing I did in my twenty years to deserve what has happened to me in this war."

Several months before I arrived in Sarajevo, Renata attempted to talk to her parents through ham radio operators but was unable to speak with them directly. She says, "That's the day I wanted to tell them I was pregnant. I was afraid I might die and thought it was better to tell them through a stranger than for them to never know. So I told the radio operator to please tell my parents I'm pregnant. Tell them I'm a different person now than I was when they left. I tried to explain to the ham operator why I was having a baby. Before the war, I was afraid of having a baby, but everything changed in the war. I grew up fast. It was strange. I could hear my mother, but she couldn't hear me. My mother said, 'What! She's pregnant! No! She's not pregnant.' Then the radio operator said, 'Yes, your daughter is pregnant and you will soon be a grandmother.' "

Like most people outside Sarajevo during the siege, Renata's parents, although they were from Sarajevo, could never fully understand that the aggressor on the mountains had taken everyone in the city hostage. During the next two years, Renata's parents repeatedly ask me to beg their daughter to "Take a bus to Belgrade." But there was no bus to Belgrade, and even if there was, Renata said, "My mother is Serbian and my father Muslim. My husband is Muslim. Because of my last name, I am afraid to leave by a convoy and travel through Serbian checkpoints."

She said, "My parents don't understand I am unable to even travel to the other side of the city, the side held by the aggressor. I cannot just cross the bridge and say to the aggressor, 'Okay, Renata is coming. I have nothing against you, but I want to leave Sarajevo. I want to go to Serbia. Please will you let me through?' The aggressor will kill me." As much as Renata's parents and I want her out of Sarajevo, she remains in the city until literally the final hours of the war.

On one of my visits to Sarajevo toward the end of the war, Renata says to me, "The first time you came here, everything changed for me. Because of your presence, I had hope for the future. I knew you were not able to stop the killing, but you brought news from my parents and kept coming back bringing us help. Before you came, I had nothing to believe in. It was hard all the time. But when you brought food and money from my parents, I felt hopeful again.

"It was enough when you came the first time because you didn't know how it was here. But when you came again and again, you knew the conditions. Usually people sit and feel sorry for the people they see on television who are starving, but will not try to do anything. Maybe they don't realize what happened here can happen anywhere!"

Renata, February 1994
Photo: Linda Beekman

~ CHAPTER FIVE ~
SUMMER IN THE SIEGE, 1993

Less than a week after our arrival in Sarajevo, Anne and I move from our ninth-floor Sniper Alley pinnacle to Renata's three-bedroom second-floor apartment. I call it Renata's apartment, but her parents in the United States still own it. When I met her parents in Florida before I left home, they insisted I stay in their apartment and when I met Renata, she did too.

Located on a tiny street near the edge of the Bascarsija, a part of the city built during the Ottoman Empire, this modern four-story building, complete with marble stairs, offers the illusion of safety because it does not face the mountain. It sits sandwiched between the shelter of several taller buildings; however, wide silver duct tape holds the glass in the living room bay window together and neighbors tell me the roof received a direct mortar hit.

This city continues to amaze me. Many hardships I had prepared to encounter have not materialized. In the apartment, I expect only a place on the floor to throw my sleeping bag. Instead, I find an immaculately clean bedroom with a freshly made bed waiting for me. I am horrified to learn Renata and her sister-in-law made the dangerous hour walk from her mother-in-law's apartment the day before to prepare the apartment for our stay.

Our new accommodations feel safer than Jana's apartment, plus the building often has running water in the basement—sometimes even a trickle makes it upstairs. Sarajevo's water supply originates from springs on Trebevic Mountain. The enemy, situated on the mountain, also needs water and cannot totally control it just for themselves. Some water escapes and flows down through the pipes from the mountain and into a few buildings positioned by chance in the right locations. Usually there is not enough pressure to push the water upstairs, but at least on most days we are spared the dangerous trek across the river to the brewery to collect water. During the day, a steady stream of neighbors descends to the basement to fill their containers. Even our visitors bring empty containers because they know there may be running water in the basement.

Our bathtub is always filled to the brim and serves as a reservoir. On shelves around the tub, miscellaneous old plastic soft drink and wine bottles stand filled. Next to the toilet, a large plastic crock, usually used to store pickled cabbage during the winter months, serves as another reservoir. Various other containers sit on the floor in the smaller hall bathroom and in the kitchen.

Anne and I share the apartment with Renata's husband's older brother, Jagger (a nickname inherited from the time Mick Jagger performed in Sarajevo and everyone said they looked alike). Renata and her husband will not return to live in the apartment until after the birth of their baby.

Jagger, a tall, gentle, burly guy with a chiseled face, barely tolerates the role of soldier. Dressed in jeans now two sizes too big and an antique gun tucked in his belt, he reluctantly climbs the hill above our neighborhood several times a week to fight on the front line. Often, he returns exhausted and muddy from head to foot, but clutching a bunch of wild red roses, picked for Anne and me on his way down the mountain.

Like Renata's husband, Jagger is a Muslim. Early in the war, he sent his Serbian wife and their small child to Serbia to live with her family. Eventually their marriage will become one of the many casualties of the war.

Jagger is not an emancipated male. With the stress of confronting mortars and sniper fire, I decide I haven't the strength to uphold my feminist standards, so I relent, and join Anne in assuming the role of caretaker. We clean, make coffee, prepare skimpy meals, and wash the dishes.

Jagger teaches us how to make a fire in the #10 tin can he has propped up on three bricks on the small balcony. A small pile of wood, stacked and covered, stands in the corner. He tells us to help ourselves, but we know every piece of wood we use now will mean one less they will have this coming winter. Anne and I scrounge for anything to burn: scraps of paper, used tissues, cardboard, and even used mini sanitary pads and baby wipes, which ignite quickly because they contain alcohol.

Cooking on the tin can, I learn the real meaning of energy: how much fuel it takes to boil two cups of water, to cook two cups of rice, or to cook a cup of dried beans. The beans never thoroughly cook and bring major complaints from a local guest.

On rare days, Jagger disappears with his ration card and returns with a large loaf of bread. He carts water up from the basement and if there is no water in the building, he makes the trip across the river to the beer factory to collect water. Sometimes he escorts us around the neighborhood in the evening. One night as we walk past the beer factory, a huge pile of garbage burns nearby on the street. All of a sudden, I hear a loud explosion and, simultaneously, something hits my arm. I thought I had been shot, but it was only a tin can that had exploded in the fire.

Jagger is patient and attempts to solve our small day-to-day problems as we communicate to each other through the language of pantomime.

A neighbor later tells me that one day early in the war, she and some other neighbors were visiting Jagger when Serbs began firing special shells designed to break into thousands of pieces. She said it sounded like hundreds of guns firing, and she and the others thought the Serbs had entered the city and were fighting in the streets. She said, "Only Jagger had a gun. He was at the door. He said, 'Be calm, I will fight! I will save you all!' One gun—one man. We were terrified. We thought the enemy was in the city! We thought they were occupying us! There was Jagger, protecting us from the army of former Yugoslavia—the fourth-largest army in Europe."

In spite of the chaos of war, Anne and I quickly settle into a daily rhythm. Without electricity, we get up with the sun and go to bed at dark. I sleep unbelievably well, although my bed sways from time to time from the vibrations of mortar hits. One night, particularly heavy shelling keeps me awake. With each vibration, I realize if Serbs break through the war's front line on the ridge above our neighborhood, we will be caught in their path as they swoop down the hill in their usual door-to-door terror. They will not ask or care if we are American.

By the following morning the fear has diminished, and Anne and I build a small fire in the tin can to boil two cups of water to make coffee. Our diet consists of small servings of crackers, canned tuna, jam, processed cheese, dried fruit, instant cereal, and bread—usually flat bread made in a frying pan, or a doughnut-like Bosnian bread fried in oil, when we have oil. Back home I always drained tuna oil. Here, we save it to fuel lamps or use it as a substitute for butter.

We share our food with Jagger, and he shares his bread, flour, and occasional can of fish he receives as humanitarian aid. We have no choice but to drink local water purified with iodine tablets. The taste is terrible, so I add a little unsweetened Kool-Aid I brought to kill the iodine taste.

Food is a big issue, but Sarajevans rarely speak of hunger. The dining room table has been dismantled and is stored in a bedroom. No one ever eats on the street, and one rarely gives or receives a dinner invitation. Later in the summer, after I return from grocery shopping in Italy, the electricity briefly comes back on after being off for weeks. We have a party. We make pizza—with yeast dough, ketchup sauce, and sardines topped with Parmesan cheese from Italy.

One of the consequences of not having electricity is the sense of community it creates. Late every afternoon, our neighbors gather in the courtyard of our building until dark. Sometimes the old men bring out a card table and play chess. Women share the day's news and everyone tells jokes. Black humor runs rampant, with the current favorite being, "How is Sarajevo different from Auschwitz?" The answer, "Auschwitz had gas." Another favorite is about food. A woman asks, "How do you make stuffed shells?" She then says, "Boil large macaroni shells, then boil small macaroni, and put the small macaroni into the large macaroni." As the women laugh, children run and play after being cooped up all day. Young teens, especially the girls, stand off by themselves sharing their secrets.

One twelve-year-old boy with a vacant stare ignores the other children and clings to his mother. His hair is short and his head scarred. His mother says before the shrapnel hit him, he was outgoing and at the top of his class. Now, he only wants to stay by her side.

The first time the electricity comes on it feels strange. Darkness is the only way I have known Sarajevo. Surprisingly, the first sound I hear from the television is a James Bond movie. For several days, the TV continues to blare and each evening the courtyard remains silent, because TV offers an escape from the reality of war. But soon the darkness returns and the televisions are silenced, reminding everyone the war is still with us.

More than a week after our arrival, Anne and I remain the only members of the peace initiative to reach Sarajevo. Every day we visit local organizations and government offices to solicit support for the peace camps. Because there is no transportation, it isn't possible to accomplish much. Without telephone service, one can't call ahead for appointments. So, like everyone else, we just drop in, and whether the person is head of a company, an organization, or the mayor, they usually stop what they are doing and see us. If something doesn't get done today, we wait until tomorrow. If appointments are made, it is with the unspoken understanding that "no shows" are acceptable because war is unpredictable.

Each day we attempt to make short-wave radio contact with Padova. This means a trek across town through dangerous intersections to one of the half-destroyed Unis towers—Sarajevo's tallest buildings. There, on one of the intact, unburned floors, a French organization operates a short-wave radio service so locals can contact relatives in other parts of the world. The walk there, the time spent waiting in line, and the walk back takes between two and three hours. The young French woman running the project lives there. I feel concerned for her safety, because in an adjoining room, she stores gallons of fuel used to run the generator.

Finally, after many attempts we make contact with Padova. Within several days, several members of our group start to trickle into the city. The first is a saintly Spaniard, Herardo, who leads our group in delivering mail to the most dangerous parts of the city. (Mail brought to Split by the two-thousand Europeans and other activists from many parts of the world that hope to participate in the peace camps in August. The letters and packages are from Bosnian refugees living abroad, and sent to their families and friends still in Sarajevo.) Soon, the Italians arrive, Luca, Pascal, Gigi, Filippo, Federico, and Luigi—all human rights activists who have worked on issues within Italy and in other places such as South Africa. Later in the summer, others come, including two young Italian women. They all find accommodations in a dilapidated hotel near the main square in the Bascarsija. Anne and I decide not to move there, but remain living in Renata's apartment. As soon as the group settles in, we meet them at the hotel every evening for several hours to organize our work toward creating the peace camps. Anne and I always leave the meeting at ten minutes to nine, because curfew is at nine. Anyone caught on the street after that time is detained overnight by the police.

In late July 1993, two new members of our group are in Ancona waiting to fly in but need flak jackets. I volunteer to fly out to shuttle our extra jackets to them, because once members arrive in Sarajevo they don't use the jackets. I know my friend Edith Daly, from Florida, is part of the large group in Ancona, and I want to help her get a press card so she can come to Sarajevo via the airlift.

I fly to Split, take the ferry to Ancona and find the larger Beati group, about 2,000 people, gathered in a warehouse waiting to begin their journey to Sarajevo to set up the peace camps. The following evening everyone boards a chartered ferry to cross the Adriatic Sea. Many large multi-colored Italian flags with the Italian word *pace* (peace) wave in the breeze. When we dock at Split the next morning, I whisk Edith away to the press office at the airport to follow the path I took less than a month ago. She has faxed her letter from the States claiming she is a journalist. In several hours, we are both on a plane headed for Sarajevo.

In another week, it is clear the Beati organization cannot accomplish its peace mission. I am not surprised. The Serbs' attack on Sarajevo has not let up. The 2,000 peace activists are caught somewhere on the road from Split to Sarajevo. In normal times, the drive is five to six hours. They have been creeping along in buses for four days, negotiating numerous checkpoints and camping by the side of the road at night. The United Nations has sent ultimatum after ultimatum requiring the Serbs to withdraw their weapons in and around Sarajevo or face NATO air strikes, but the Serbs do not budge and neither does NATO.

The situation reminds me of a verse Walt Whitman wrote 100 years ago in his anthology of poems, *Leaves of Grass:*

> *What place is besieged, and vainly tries to raise the siege?*
> *Lo, I send to that place a commander, swift, brave, immortal.*
> *And with him horse and foot, and parks of artillery,*
> *And artillery-men, the deadliest that ever fired gun.*

For now, there will be no parks of artillery for Bosnia—only the embargo on weapons and the erratic delivery of humanitarian aid.

I came to Sarajevo believing I am a pacifist, but now I join Sarajevans in hoping for NATO air strikes. I believe NATO has the capability to bomb the tanks and weapons on the mountains surrounding Sarajevo without killing anyone if they give the aggressor ample time to leave before the attack. Civilians in Sarajevo are hostages in their own homes. The attackers have cut the electricity, water, and food supply, and bombard residents daily with mortars and sniper fire. They deliberately shoot children. Sarajevans deserve to be helped or at least allowed to defend themselves. The one time in my life I am in favor of U.S. intervention, it does not come.

I have voluntarily placed myself in this city under siege. I face the same constant threat of death as everyone else, only I have a press card—a ticket out if the airport is open and the airlift operating. My neighbors here do not enjoy this escape valve. Before the siege, they freely traveled in and out of their city. Now, not all want to leave, but not having the option almost drives them mad.

With great disappointment, members of our Beati group retrace our steps to tell the local organizations we have visited that the peace camps will not take place. We had all hoped several thousand activists arriving in the city would at least temporarily stop the fighting and maybe set a precedent for civilian intervention in war.

Several days later, we are shocked when a group of about eight people arrives in Sarajevo. Determined to get through, they broke off from the main Beati group and negotiated their way through Serb lines. They are permitted to stay only forty-eight hours. Among them is an American, Willa Elam.

Our Beati group continues to meet every night to determine how we can be of help in the city. One important task is the delivery of hundreds of letters the members of the large group carried, sent from Bosnians outside Sarajevo to their relatives and friends. There is no government mail service during the war. Another Beati project is to bring in via the airlift the food packages the larger group would have brought overland had they made it. For now, the mail and food are stored in a Catholic church in Ancona.

Edith and I continue to work with Beati, but we also have another agenda—get Renata evacuated on the airlift. Anne decides her work in Sarajevo is almost finished and soon returns to the United States.

On Aug. 6, 1993, Renata gives birth to a son. She says, "He is the only good thing that happened to me in this war." On her final pre-natal visit, the hospital instructs her to bring three liters of water and a flashlight when she comes to deliver. (Edith and I provide the flashlight.)

After the delivery, she sits on the side of her bed for more than an hour without pain medication, waiting for the doctor to stitch her episiotomy. Later, both she and the baby develop infections. The condition of the baby is not clear. His lips are blue, his skin yellow, and his breathing seems irregular, but the day following the birth, they are both discharged and return to Renata's husband's family, where she and the baby stay inside for forty days. It is the Muslim custom after the birth of a baby—to protect the mother and baby from infections. Renata and her husband name the baby Haris, after a good friend who was best man at their wedding—a friend blown apart in the trenches by an enemy shell.

Several weeks later the baby is back in the hospital for several days for tests of his heart, but the electricity is never on long enough to complete the process. Lack of electricity is only one of many severe problems the hospital staff lives with. Because there is no running water, large plastic containers resembling water mattresses line the halls. A water truck delivers water to the hospital and pumps it to the upper floors. One day, I see a young woman cleaning the stairs with a muddy rag. She wears no gloves. On the streets surrounding the hospital, large dumpsters overflow with bloody bandages and other contaminated waste. But what the hospital lacks due to war conditions, the staff makes up for through sheer dedication. Most doctors and staff work without a salary or for fewer than several German marks a month—less than five dollars. In addition to illness and injuries caused by the war, individuals suffer from ordinary illnesses encountered in every society.

Renata is not alone in choosing to affirm life in war by having a baby. A baby boom in Sarajevo astonishes the local and international community. A local radio station announces daily the number of babies born the previous day.

One day about a month after I arrive in Sarajevo, Renata says to me, "Since you are here is the first time since the war began that I haven't been hungry." To know I stand between her and hunger stuns me. This awareness drives me for the next two years to do all I can to help sustain her and the baby with material aid and to attempt to evacuate them from Sarajevo.

Edith and I swing into action. In a humanitarian organization we discover a fax machine, part of a phone system called the Pittsburgh Line. A very sympathetic person there gives us permission to use it. Years later, I heard their phone bill stretched into tens of thousand of dollars—but not all from our faxes! The satellite system was routed through the United States, so we only needed dial 1, then the area code and number. Every other day, we fax friends and government officials back home asking them to petition the United Nations High Commissioner for Refugees representative in Washington, D.C., and President Clinton to help Renata. We constantly make rounds in Sarajevo to UNHCR and any other agency we feel might have the authority to evacuate Renata and the baby.

Our efforts to help Renata often take us to the Holiday Inn, since the war began, home to many journalists and the American ambassador. It's a foolish place to visit because the building faces Sniper Alley. Our approach is on foot from a building in back, a fifty-meter dash through an open field. We do not enjoy the protection of armored personnel carriers, as journalists from network media do. I don't know why we think running will avoid a sniper's bullet.

In late August, after such a trip to the Holiday Inn, we walk back toward Renata's apartment. The day is sunny and quiet; pedestrians crowd the sidewalks. As we reach the center of town, I think, "Only ten more minutes and we are home."

Unexpectedly, two sharp sounds—*ping, ping*—pierce my illusion of security. We all freeze. My eyes search for the victim. I find him slumped on the pavement of a small path in the park across the street. In what seems like time frozen, a car careens through the park. A passenger jumps out and throws the victim into the back seat. The car speeds away up the hill toward Kosevo Hospital.

In the next moment, as if a director yelled "action," we all start running like ants disturbed in their nest. Two thoughts haunt me: "Is he dead?" and "I walked across that very spot a dozen times since I came to Sarajevo." That evening, in our courtyard, our neighbors tell us the young man is dead.

At one point, Edith and I are so desperate to help Renata and the baby we fly to Ancona and take a train to Geneva to plead our case in person to U.N. officials. It does not help. We return with our packs stuffed with food, a few violin strings for the Sarajevo String Quartet, and cigarettes donated by an owner of a shop in Geneva when he heard we were on our way back to Sarajevo.

Flying in and out of the city is always a risk. The threat of Serb gunfire is always present. As the airlift planes enter Bosnian Serb territory, passengers and crew are required to put on their flak jackets. It is also possible that, for security reasons, the airport in Sarajevo will close or the airlift will shut down due to mechanical problems or heavy fighting on the ground. Each time I plan to fly in or out of Sarajevo I always know the planes might not fly or I might get stranded in Sarajevo or in Italy.

On Sept. 10, Edith and I sadly say our final goodbyes in Sarajevo and return to Padova to pick up the clothes that I ditched while packing in July. Once back in civilization, we see such abundance in the shops and grocery stores, we can only think of Renata and our other friends in Sarajevo living without adequate necessities. We look at each other and decide to return one more time to bring supplies and make one last attempt at an evacuation for Renata and Haris.

We fly back to Sarajevo and when we arrive back at the apartment, we find Renata, her husband, and the baby now living there. Her husband is back, but not for long; usually he is on the front line several days at a time.

It is mid-September and already very cold. One rainy evening, Edith, Renata, the baby, and I are in the apartment. The electricity is off so we all take refuge in our beds because we can't deal with the cold or the darkness. Renata puts the baby in bed with her. After several hours she jumps up shrieking, "Where is he? I can't find him! I can't find him!" In the darkness, she gropes for her screaming baby, who has become tangled in the blankets and has slid onto the floor. In tears and desperation she cries, "I hate this stupid war! I hate it!"

Renata's life revolves around keeping her baby fed, warm, and clean. Her thoughts are always on the next shipment of humanitarian aid. She and another young mother in the neighborhood often share to make it to the next shipment. As the weather turns cold, Renata's hands quickly become chapped from washing diapers in ice-cold water.

During these last few days in Sarajevo, I feel an urgency to leave the city and return home. I feel my luck in this war zone is running out. We hit a brick wall in our final attempt to evacuate Renata and the baby, so the most we can do is scour the city one last time for food and supplies to leave with our friends. By some good luck, we find a French PX at the airport and buy as much canned meat and Nescafe as we can afford and can carry. A large jar of Nescafe still sells on the black market for about sixty dollars. Renata and her husband can sell or barter what they don't need for other supplies.

Once again Edith and I say goodbye and hitch a ride to the airport. I cry the whole flight back to Ancona—hurting for the friends I leave behind in Sarajevo. It's almost three months since I said goodbye to my own son. Living in war has afforded me little time to think of him, and I cry for this too. I am tired and feel defeated at leaving Renata and the baby behind. I don't look forward to her parents' disappointment when they meet us at the airport in Tampa. But little do I know my return home will not mark an end, but a beginning. I journey from the United States to Sarajevo four more times during the siege and another five times after the Dayton Peace Agreement is signed.

As I settle into being home, I receive the news that a member of the Beati group, an Italian, Gabriele Moreno Locatelli, was shot and killed in Sarajevo on Vrbanja bridge, where the first victim of the war was killed. Moreno had arrived in Sarajevo only a few days before Edith and I left. His death depresses me for weeks and moves me to seriously consider whether I will ever return to the city. But injustice in Bosnia brought Moreno to Sarajevo, the same as it did me. In a little more than four months, I return.

Renata
Vjecnica - Burned National Library
Photo: Jay Craig

~ Chapter Six ~

February 1994—Town Refugees

The tank-taxi rolls to a stop by the river. I feel lucky the driver agreed to let me out fewer than 100 meters from Renata's apartment. I slush by mounds of snow dunes narrowing the street. As I approach her building, I notice the doorbell buttons are dark—no electricity. I move below her second-floor bay window and call, "Renata, it's Linda!" She swings opens the window and with a broad smile, cries, "You're back!" She throws me the key, and I feel as though I have come home.

It's almost a week since I left Florida. On the day I left, Serbs fired a 120-mm high-explosive mortar into the main outdoor marketplace in Sarajevo, killing and wounding dozens of vendors and Saturday shoppers. When I arrive in Zagreb the next day I hear the news.

After returning home from my first trip to Sarajevo last fall in 1993, I constantly struggled with thoughts of returning to the besieged city. The death of Beati member Moreno Locatelli caused me to consider more realistically the dangers. Going back meant I would be returning alone and I didn't know if I could handle the logistics of the trip. My press card expired at the end of December. Departing before then would have been easy, but would not have given me enough time to collect supplies and funds for my return trip. By waiting until now, in February 1994, I was forced to make a dreaded side trip to Zagreb—now the only U.N. office issuing press cards. For journalists with expense accounts, the stop to get press cards is a small annoyance. For me, operating on a shoestring budget and lugging two fifty-pound wheeled suitcases filled with diapers, baby food, vitamins, batteries, dried fruit, nuts, and other food, the side trip to Zagreb, and then on to Ancona via an overnight train through Croatia and Italy with two train changes is a nightmare. In addition to the problem of travel logistics, the radio station in Tampa, which the previous summer had permitted me to represent it in order to get my U.N. press card, withdrew its support out of fear of possible liability if I got hurt or was killed. I had to find another media organization to represent.

As a Floridian who didn't own a heavy coat or a pair of boots, I dreaded the thought of three weeks of Bosnian winter without electricity. But my fears for Renata and her baby still living in war outweighed my concerns.

After several weeks of wavering, I paste an affirmation in my checkbook: "I am willing and able and have all the money I need to return to Sarajevo." I believed if preparations for the journey went well, it would be a sign I was meant to return.

In late October 1993, I attend a meeting of The Tampa Bay Peace Education Program, a project of The St. Petersburg Friends Meeting (Quakers), and ask if I can organize a project within their group for the purpose of collecting funds and supplies for another trip to Sarajevo. They agree and I name the project *The Sarajevo Project*. At this point, my vision is for one more trip to Sarajevo in February 1994. I do not realize my commitment to Sarajevo will grow, support for the project will mushroom, and that I will return to Sarajevo eight more times after this February trip.

In addition to raising money and supplies for the trip, I also need a flak jacket—mandatory gear needed for passage on the airlift. Last summer on my first trip to Sarajevo, the Beati organization provided me one. Now, returning alone, I had to supply my own. The cheapest model cost several hundred dollars new. I found a used one in an Army/Navy store, but it was so flimsy I could have recreated it from a yard of cotton fabric and tin foil, which at one point I considered doing. Finally, I went to the St. Petersburg Police Department to ask if I could place a notice on their employee bulletin board advertising to buy a used flak jacket. The clerk at the desk said, "Wait just a minute and someone will speak with you." Soon a police officer came up the stairs with a flak jacket rolled up in his hands. He looked at me and said, "Here, wear it in good health." Stunned, I said, "Thank you." He disappeared down the stairs. The spirit has spoken: "You will to return to Bosnia." I knew from that point on I would receive everything I needed to return to Sarajevo.

My friend Edith Daly decided not to return to Sarajevo but supported preparations for my journey. She made a new black cover for the jacket with deep hidden pockets for smuggling letters past U.N. officials at the airport, both in Ancona and Sarajevo. She also added several large inside pockets to the winter jacket I borrowed from my son.

The preparations at home for the journey went well, but it is even smoother in Zagreb. A friend of Renata's father in Florida contacted a family he knew in Zagreb and asked them to meet me and put me up for the night, which they did. The following morning they drove me to the press office and within a half-hour I emerged with a new press card. Again, I am a journalist. At two in the afternoon I take a train headed to Italy. I change trains twice in the night and arrive in Ancona at six in the morning. I immediately take the bus to the airport. With the bombing of the marketplace a few days ago, I wonder if the airport in Sarajevo is open. Twenty-five journalists from all corners of the world are ahead of me on the transport list. The marketplace massacre is big news. The airport is open, but one airlift plane is not operating, so the chances of getting into Sarajevo on this day are slim. Journalists do not have priority on the airlift, and many times the planes only permit three or four passengers at a time. At 2:30 in the afternoon I am still sitting in the waiting room—my name nowhere near the beginning of the list. I call it a day and return to Ancona to find a room for the night. The following day is the same, and I do not get on a plane. On the second night at the hotel I ask the manager if I can store one suitcase there for a few days. I plan to return to Ancona to get it several days after I arrive in Sarajevo. I know my luggage is over the 30-kilo limit and, after waiting two days to get on a plane, I don't want to risk annoying U.N. personnel when they weigh my luggage. On the third day I am lucky; I board a plane in the late morning and arrive in Sarajevo a little after noon.

The city has not changed much in four months except fresh snow now hides the garbage and some of the destruction. I quickly realize the marketplace killings have wounded the spirits of everyone, including Renata. A dark cloud hangs over the city. She says, "Last Saturday, my husband's youngest brother had just returned from market when we heard the blast. It is only six blocks away. In that moment, something died in all of us; there are no words to describe how we feel. We never believed this could happen; Sarajevo is gray and quiet as a graveyard." A few days later when vendors return to sell in the same marketplace, Renata is distraught because they resume their business in the place where so many died.

Although the city has not changed, Renata's apartment has. She and her husband have shifted gears to winter survival mode. A new wood-burning tin stove stands in the corner of the living room. The crib is close by, too close in my opinion. A white sheer curtain divides the living room in order to hold the heat in at the side with the stove. Two pullout sofas sit on opposite walls, one for Renata and her husband, and the other for family or guests. I opt for privacy and ask to sleep in one of the unheated bedrooms. I don't know exactly how cold it is in my bedroom, but I can always see my breath. I avoid undressing and wear all my clothes to bed, including my coat.

On one occasion, the water pipes freeze and Renata's husband goes to the basement to build a fire around the pipes to melt the ice.

Caring for the baby in freezing cold distresses Renata. He is surprisingly chubby and in better health than when I left in September. His lips are no longer blue and the severe diaper rash is gone, but she is concerned because he is six months old and not yet crawling. But how can he? By necessity, he is always bundled beyond movement and either confined to his stroller or crib. She cannot put him on the floor because it is drafty and impossible to keep clean. She does stand him in a Bosnian version of a walker that supports his body in a standing position while permitting him to move by himself in a circle.

Washing diapers is also distressing. The washing machine works, but not without electricity and water. She boils the diapers in a large pot on the wood stove and then rinses them in icy water in the bathroom. Heating water for the rinse is extravagant. Fuel is needed for cooking. The first winter of the siege she burned her music books—Beethoven and Bach. Now, I notice the bolts of fabric from her mother's sewing cabinet are missing.

I unpack the diaper cream, baby vitamins, baby clothes, and the teddy bear her parents sent. They also have sent money. The Quakers in Florida have donated dried fruit, nuts, cheese, baby food, powered milk, batteries, candles, first aid supplies, and funds for Renata and others. A Bosnian in Florida asked me to deliver money to three of his relatives. Renata's aunt, a refugee in England, sent me money to take to her elderly parents. Renata laughs and says, "When you come here, it's like Christmas!"

In addition to the supplies for Renata, I also bring answers to dozens of children's pen-pal letters a Bosnian group called Flowers of Love (Cvijece Ljubavi) gave me last summer to deliver to children in Florida. Among the letters is one from my fifteen-year-old son to a girl named Irma. I know Irma's letter well because during the past four months I often read it to audiences in the United States when I spoke about Sarajevo. Just before this trip, I realized I had not found a pen pal for Irma, so I asked my son if he would like to write to her.

After Irma receives my son's letter, she realizes I am staying in the same neighborhood where she lives. She sends her older sister Selma to invite me to their apartment. Finally, I will meet this teenager whose letter moves me to tears each time I read it.

The next evening, Irma and her sister Selma come to escort me through the snowy passageway from Renata's building to their apartment on the next street. The foyer and stairway of their building are dark and grimy. The building has never recovered from the fire next door, and a strong, sickening odor lingers in the hall. It disturbs me; maybe it is the smell of burned flesh.

As I enter their top floor apartment, I immediately remember my visit several years ago to the Anne Frank House in Amsterdam—the upper rooms where Anne Frank and her family hid from the Nazis. Anne and Irma, two teenagers of different faiths—Anne, Jewish, Irma, Muslim—both caught in wars a half-century apart, yet their enemy is the same: genocide.

Before Irma and her family became refugees in their own town, they lived in a suburb of Sarajevo. There on March 3, 1992, they began their journey in this war when a five a.m. phone call startled Irma and Selma from their sleep. The call was for their father; a guard at the company in Sarajevo where he worked broke the news, "Masked gunmen, Serb nationalists, have barricaded the city! The town is dead! No one is on the street! Don't come to work today! Don't leave your house!"

The call marked the end of Irma's childhood and the end of her family's idyllic life in their suburban dream home.

The fear on her father's face terrifies Irma, then just thirteen, and she cries hysterically. She waits for a knock on the door, sure someone is coming to kill her parents. She has heard "bad stories" about war in Croatia and in other parts of Bosnia, but she never thought it could happen in Sarajevo. But in the months before the phone rang, the family began sensing an atmosphere of intolerance creeping into their city, a subtle, unspoken pressure or force implying, "It is wrong for people of different ethnic groups or religions to live together. It is wrong to respect each other's differences."

Distraught with the news from the phone call, Irma withdraws to her bed and writes a poem, "Don't Ruin Our Peace," a song of fear, a song of prayer—not to God, but to the Serbs, asking them to stop. She wants her parents to live. She wants to live. She wants a future.

You, sick minds
who use common people's suffering to satisfy dirty desires,
You made me write this poem.

You shallow minds
who can't even imagine what real life is all about.
You, who make children cry, day and night.

Hear our prayers!
We never wanted this war to happen.
Put your guns down and let us live like we used to.

You cowards,
One day you will gather to make agreements towards peace.
By then, many people will be gone forever.

So, I say,
"Put your guns away!
Be reasonable!
Don't ruin our peace."

In response to the barricades and gunmen, Sarajevans initially locked themselves in their homes, but later on that March day they poured out into the streets in solidarity for a multi-ethnic Bosnia. The gunmen backed down and removed the barricades. Sarajevans thought they had won; they believed the threat was gone.

Life returned to normal, and Irma wrote a new poem:

Spring is in the Air
It comes from somewhere far away
Slowly sneaking up on us.
It wakes us up, and we say,
"Spring is in the air."

High in the mountains
the wind carries it on its wings.
All people are joyful
when they feel spring sing.

Brought with the wind
It brings a present to everyone without exception.
It knocks on everyone's door giving its wonderful possession.
And so it stays for some time
Until it's ready to leave for some other place.

It says good-bye until next year
And leaves us with a smile on its beautiful face.

In addition to the advent of spring, Serb nationalists quietly arrive and entrench tons of military vehicles and weapons on the hills and mountains surrounding Sarajevo.

On April 6, again brandishing guns and wearing stocking masks, Serb nationalists return, setting up new barricades, annexing parts of the city. That day, thousands of Sarajevans—Muslims, Croats, and Serbs—gather near Parliament for a "Peace and Unity" demonstration. In the bright sun, musicians play and journalists document support for an independent, united, and diverse Bosnia.

As Irma watches the demonstration on television, she falls asleep on the sofa. Soon, her parents' cries of, "Oh my God!" startle her from her nap. Snipers fired into the crowd. The aggressor claims its first victim: Suada Dilberović, a medical student from Dubrovnik, Croatia. Her dying words are reported to have been: "Oh, please do not tell me this is happening in Sarajevo." The wounded, crying for help, are scattered on the street. "Am I having a bad dream?" Irma asks. "I fall asleep in peace, but wake up to war. Now, the sun is gone. It is raining."

During the next several hours, Irma and her family sit stunned as they learn that masked killers have dug and occupy trenches, cutting off Grbavica, a large neighborhood across the river from the Holiday Inn. Military planes from the former Yugoslav army, controlled by Belgrade (the capital of Serbia and former Yugoslavia), take off from the military airport just outside Sarajevo and fly low, rattling windows—threatening, warning.

That night from their second-floor bathroom window, Irma and her family witness the aggressor, nationalist Serbs on Trebevic Mountain, shooting shells into downtown Sarajevo. "I am so afraid," Irma says. "The shells light up the sky and turn it red. There is smoke. It is the worst night of my life. I fear they will attack us in the night. I knew if this was happening in Sarajevo, all of Bosnia was ruined."

In the next few days, Irma's parents live in denial. Schools are closed, but they leave their children home while they travel about four miles into Sarajevo to work. They return with news about the destruction of the town.

In shock, they all hold on to the hope that war will not come to their suburban neighborhood. (Many Sarajevans told me that in 1991, when the war started in Slovenia, and then Croatia, they stuck their head in the sand. War was at their back door, but they said to themselves, "War is over there, it will not affect me, it will not come here.")

During the next twenty days, Irma's father sheds twenty pounds. He fears the dark cloud engulfing Sarajevo might devour his family. He confides in his oldest daughter, Selma, about the possibility of the enemy targeting him, because he holds an important position in his firm. He fears for his family if something happens to him.

His fears are well grounded. Several months later, a sniper shoots him in the thigh as he crosses the street near his company. On the same day, they kill his friend and colleague. Eventually, staff at his company discover a "hit list" with his name on it. The list also contains the names of Serbs who do not support the aggression precipitated by the ideology of Belgrade for a "Greater Serbia." Nationalist Serbs want Serbia to absorb all of Bosnia. They do not want ethnic or religious diversity in Bosnia.

Selma later learns when the aggressor took over the neighborhood of Grbavica and other areas, troops went door to door rounding up non-Serbs. In one high-rise apartment building they sealed off all the entrances, then began their door-to-door terror searches. First, they separated the men from the women and children. On one floor, a Serbian man came out of his apartment and asked why they were persecuting the others. The masked murderers said nothing, but opened fire with a machine gun, killing the man.

Irma describes the days following April 6, the day the barricades went up and shots were fired into the crowd. She says: "There was no shooting in our neighborhood, but we felt an evil silence. Our neighbors told us to darken our windows, so we covered them with blankets. The lonely sound of dogs barking and our fear of dying almost drove us crazy. We started sleeping with our clothes on in case we needed to leave in the middle of the night."

Some neighbors offer Irma's father a gun, and ask him to go with them to organize a defense of their area. "I cannot operate a gun," he protests. "It is something stronger than me." He tells his neighbors, "I'll go with you to help, but don't give me a gun." Instead, they tell him to stay with his family.

A few days later, he reinforces the front door of their house with boards. He knows if the killers come, they will rape, torture, and murder his family. Irma says, "He told me much later, after we escaped from that situation, if the masked killers had come to the house, he was prepared to kill us and then himself."

Irma's father is intelligent, thoughtful, responsible, kind, lovingly strict, and always considering the best for his three daughters. Although he and I were born in the same year, in his presence I feel I am a fourth daughter.

Irma and her family continue to fear an unknown enemy. Irma says, "On April 25, we decide to leave our house and go to my grandmother's apartment about two miles away. We don't plan to leave forever, only until things get better—until we feel safer. My grandmother's apartment is in the newer part of Sarajevo with blocks of high-rise apartment buildings designed with a field or park in the center. Although the aggressor is already bombing that area, we feel we will be safer there among a larger population than in our small, isolated neighborhood. Serbs have already ethnically cleansed and destroyed similar villages and suburbs in Bosnia, and we don't want to be home when they come to our door."

Irma says, "I begin cramming necessities into my rucksack; I look around my room. I feel dizzy, helpless and miserable—I want to take it all with me. Unconsciously I begin tidying up my room. I want to know everything is okay, but something is breaking my heart. I don't want to turn off the song on my record player."

Who knows? Maybe there's another world waiting for me?
Who knows? Sometimes in the darkness springs up a beautiful flower.
Maybe, Who knows?
Maybe, one of the luckiest, one in a thousand I will be!

"I turn off the music. I don't realize this is my last day in my house, as I have known it as a child."

As she steps out the door of her home, Irma doesn't know she has become a refugee, an experience that will leave her yearning for her future, for something good to happen. When I meet Irma she tells me, "Before the war, I was satisfied with my life. Everything good was with me every day. I didn't have a need to long for something else. War has taken a sense of completeness away. Now I feel the need to catch up with life, but I can't."

After leaving their house, Irma's parents and her maternal grandmother returned there every two or three days to pick up clean clothes and to work in their vegetable garden. After one such trip on May 26, they head back to Sarajevo on foot. Halfway back, three Serbian soldiers stop them and tell them they cannot pass. Irma's father pleads with them—explaining his children are alone in Sarajevo. Finally, the soldiers let them go, but warn them never to come back. Irma's parents and grandmother turn and walk toward Sarajevo, never looking back.

Two days later, Serbs from the Yugoslav army barracks near Irma's home attack the neighborhood. The presence of the barracks had always consoled Irma's parents; no one ever dreamed the National Army would attack its own people. Now it was these very soldiers, Serb nationalists who have taken over the Yugoslav army, who burn, rape, and drive Irma's neighbors from their homes.

Irma and her family live in her grandmother's two-room apartment for two months, along with an aunt and her Serbian husband and their young son. During the first two days, shelling is so heavy they take refuge in the basement. Irma writes another poem:

Spring in the Basement:
We know it's spring
When the birds sing their beautiful song
When flowers blossom and grass turns green
Spring doesn't know about the words:
Suffering, pain, and scream.

Streets are not supposed to be empty
All we feel is fear.
The air smells like burned candles
There seems no way out of here.

I don't want to live in chains
And be a stranger in my own town.

Irma's grandmother's building has ten floors. One day during severe shelling, everyone takes shelter in the basement, but a shell hits and all the glass from the top floor down falls through the elevator shaft into the basement, covering everyone below. After that, the family stays in the apartment during shelling, taking shelter in a hallway.

In the next three months, Irma and her family moved three more times, each time inching closer to the center of Sarajevo and each time living with friends or relatives, ten to thirteen people in a one- or two-room apartment. One shelter was only a few yards from the front line in Grbavica.

"We lived there a month," says Irma. "The front line was just across the street from us. It was horrible! One morning we came up out of the basement where we slept, to eat breakfast. A shell exploded outside, in front of the window. We all fell to the floor covered in dust and glass. The five of us shared the place with my father's cousin's family, their two boys, their friend, and her husband and two children. We had no candles, but we made lamps with oil. One morning we spilled the oil all over us. It smelled so bad. All the time, my mother had to watch my baby sister who was almost three and didn't understand what was happening. She only wanted to go outside to play."

One day, Irma's mother receives word her husband has been shot. She frantically walks to three hospitals and clinics before she finds him. He survives. That evening, she returns to their current residence, the apartment of a Serbian friend, with her husband's bloody clothes. Her host makes an obscene joke about the torn pants, and she realizes it is not safe for them to stay there. In a few days, they move again.

Around that time, an old Serbian friend, now a soldier in the aggressor's army sends a message to Selma, Irma's older sister. He says, "I was in your house and in the rubble, I found your picture albums. I will send them to you." In a few days, she receives the package. It is a kindness, she says, they will never forget.

By September, the family moves into an empty, but vulnerable, top-floor apartment. It was spring when they left their house. Now they are facing their first winter in war, without coats, sweaters, or boots. They are grateful that friends give them some clothes, but Selma says wearing someone else's hand-me-down underwear, without first being able to wash it, is the ultimate humiliation.

Irma cries when she receives a badly torn sweater. Her mother tells her to take a needle and thread and repair it. She does, and she and Selma share it, their only sweater, for the entire winter.

During the summer of 1993, Flowers of Love, a local children's organization, invites young people to write pen-pal letters in hopes the international community will deliver them to children in their respective countries. Irma writes:

Ciao,

My name is Irma. I am writing to you from the half dark room of the most sorrowful part of the world. This is a town without chances to live. It is forbidden to exist here. Can you guess? I'm talking about the town called Olympic Sarajevo. This is the town to which happiness has said good-bye and all the world has sent to a dead hell. This is because people in the world do not want to know the truth about here. But we are here and well aware of the truth. So please come and visit us and ask, "WHY?" I am fourteen and attend war school. For more that a half a year, I did not go to school. Now many students attend war schools at great risk.

I am a refugee from the suburbs of Sarajevo. I am a town refugee. Maybe that sounds odd but the aggressor's soldiers occupy one part of the town. We have escaped from one side of the river to the other side and have become city nomads. We are homeless. I have left all of my fourteen years of my childhood and happiness. I have lost the melody of my life.

Please try to imagine the ruined picture of my past and future life. Only one kilometer has divided my family and me from our home. I have the strongest desire to go there, to cross the bridge and to grasp my dear threshold, even at terrible risk!

Otherwise, I like music, films, and languages and I like to write poems. I am interested in art. Now in Sarajevo there are no cinemas because we do not have electricity. We sit night by night, already 16 months, by candlelight. If we do not have candles, we spend our evenings in complete darkness.

I hope, all of us here hope, that this town will not die. In spite of the war circumstances, many entertainments are being organized. Just going to one theater, exhibition or cultural event, we risk our own lives. But by attending these entertainments, we have overcome all war troubles and horrors and have survived in this way.

I also like traveling. It is extremely difficult to live under the siege of this town. It feels like we live in an open horrible tunnel. We cannot escape.

I am very distressed and depressed to realize the world's ignorance and resignation about us. Why do you civilized people of the world turn your heads from our monstrous tragedy? Tell me, Why? I wonder if you can see it? You only send resolutions one by one and after nothing happens, you keep silent and admit our horrible disappearance.

What is your opinion my dear friend? Do you think us to be unworthy to be saved? Do you think we deserve death? Maybe those who have made this human disaster deserve the worst. But, why are we doomed to vanish?

I hope you are on my side of justice. If you receive my letter, read it please and if you want to know the truth about my brave people, come here and judge for yourself this unjust war.

Only one thing I ask you, please, when you turn on the lights, or water, please think of me, because I have had nothing of it for a very long time. Maybe good-bye, my unknown friend.

Irma

When Irma wrote her letter, she didn't realize it would eventually reconnect her and her family to the outside world and would influence them to leave Sarajevo.

Her letter has brought me to this tiny, narrow room where her family huddles around a small stove. There is a larger, unheated room for sleeping and an unheated kitchen and bathroom. The family seems stunned at my presence, as if they are shipwrecked on an island, and I have just arrived in a lifeboat. Like most people in Sarajevo, they are cut off from friends, family, and their former life. They feel the world has turned its back on them. Only years later will I understand the depth of their isolation.

The first thing they tell me when we meet is they have relatives in the United States who are U.S. citizens, but war has cut off all communication with them. I promise to call their family when I go to Italy in a few days to buy supplies.

As I give the international operator the number, I feel a holy responsibility. I am a link, a messenger, and a lifeline between a family trapped in war and their relatives in civilization. The phone rings and as I deliver my message there is stunned silence at the other end. The last news they had from Sarajevo was a sniper had shot Irma's father. That evening, the relatives in the United States fax guarantee letters to my hotel, assuring that if Irma and her family escape Sarajevo, they will have the necessary papers to apply for immigration to the United States.

I return to Sarajevo the following day with the faxes for Irma and her family. In addition, I bring them a small flashlight, batteries, popcorn, sugar, coffee, fresh lettuce, tomatoes, and chocolate. A few days ago while visiting the French PX I saw a bottle of wine and bought it for a rainy day. Irma and her family are Muslim and I am afraid if I offer it I will offend them, but I decide to risk it. They laugh as I pull the bottle from my backpack. We all laugh at the absurdity of this moment. Irma and her family say they are beginning to feel sane again because I have reconnected them to the "civilized world"—the world they knew before the war.

The following week, I make a second trip to Italy, and call the editor of a peace magazine in the States who provided the U.N. Press Office with a letter saying I was representing them as a journalist. I ask if he will help Irma's sister, Selma, by providing a letter saying that she, too, is representing the magazine, so she can apply for a U.N. press card. (At that time in Sarajevo, local journalists with U.N.

press cards could also fly on the airlift.) He sends me a copy of the letter by fax.

A few days after I return from Italy, I go with Selma to several offices to collect documents the press office requires for her to apply for the press card. We are tired of walking, so I suggest we catch the tank-taxi. She is hesitant because she doesn't have a press card, but I assure her I have seen local people get on, showing only what I thought was their Bosnian identity card. The tank is crowded, and we climb in. I flash my press card, and she shows her Bosnian identity card to the U.N. soldier. The door closes and we roll down the street until we come to the first Bosnian police checkpoint. The tank stops and the door opens. The guard demands to see everyone's identification. They say hers is not acceptable! I expect him to tell us to get out, but the door closes and we are off to the local police department.

My heart is pounding. What will happen? Will I lose my press card? Will she be barred from getting one? Will I be thrown out of Sarajevo? The other passengers are furious with us because we have made them late.

At the police station, I plead innocent. I don't understand what is being said and do not know a relative of Selma's family holds a high position in the police department. She isn't worried at all. In twenty minutes, they let us go. I figure we will not be allowed to continue in the tank, but they tell us to get in and off we go to the PTT. Someone tells me later, the police harassed us in order to embarrass the United Nations, whom they feel is not doing its job.

Eventually Selma receives her press card. It gives her confidence a boost, and soon she finds work in the television building. Although the rules change and she is not allowed to leave Sarajevo with the card, it is the beginning of her journey out of Sarajevo and to the United States.

I feel privileged to help Selma and her family, and others in Sarajevo—especially in the role of messenger, envoy, and intermediary, empowering them to act on their own behalf. I often ask myself why I am doing this. I do it because I figured out how to do it, and if I don't do it, who will?

One day during Ramadan, the days of fasting preceding Bajram, I visit Irma's family. It is late in the afternoon and already dark. Selma volunteers in a religious organization, delivering bread to the sick and the elderly. The bread is meant to break their day's fast, but for most, abstaining wasn't a choice. All of Sarajevo has been fasting almost for two years.

Selma rises from her chair and announces it is time for her to begin the bread delivery. As she moves through the long narrow room, she pauses to greet each family member as though she is passing through a receiving line. First, she hugs and kisses Irma. War jolted Irma from her childhood and then stole her adolescence. She is now older than her fifteen years. Next, Selma moves to her father, remembering that frantic day a sniper wounded him; they embrace. She continues towards her mother, who wears a faded blue bathrobe and bears dark circles around her eyes. Selma says, "My mother tries to make our life as normal as possible. She always brings us back to something we had before the war, even improvising cake on our birthdays. Once, she became so angry with herself, because she was saving an apple for us for a special occasion. But she hid it so well she forgot about it and it rotted." Selma wraps her arms around her mother and promises to return as soon as possible. Finally, as her four-year-old sister runs by, she grabs her and swings her into the air. They laugh. Only a baby when this war began, she has spent half of her life waiting to play outside.

As Selma moves toward me, I realize I am also part of this goodbye ceremony. She places her hands on my shoulders and kisses me gently on each cheek. Suddenly, I understand this ritual of deliberate and intentional good-byes. War has heightened her awareness—she cannot take life for granted. In the time it takes her to dash through icy streets and navigate gloomy hallways and pitch-dark stairways to distribute a few loaves of bread, any one of us could die. A wave of sorrow washes over me; I feel pain for this family trapped in this war.

War brought chaos to Selma's dreams and aspirations. Before the war, she attended the University of Sarajevo, but now she has taken on the role of caregiver to her younger sisters and sometimes to her parents. "My life is like a train passing me by," she says. "I want to catch my train."

When I meet Selma, she has already made the decision to leave Sarajevo. Our meeting rekindles her commitment to do so. Although I support her decision, I do not want to be the one to organize her departure, even if I could. It needs to come from her. The last week in February 1994, I leave Sarajevo and return to Florida. In the months following, Selma tries again and again to prepare a safe way out of the city.

In Florida, on September 13, 1994, I receive the following fax:

The United Nations will not renew my press card. Right at the time when they changed the rules and I could leave Sarajevo by a safe route, my press card has expired. It seems as if someone is playing with me. Each time I organize something, it disappears. I know you will say not to give up, but if I have to stay here one more month, I will give up. I am completely lost.

Six days later, she sends a second fax:

Today I finished work at the television building and crossed the street to the tram station, but missed the tram. Then someone called my name. It was a friend from NBC. He offered me a ride. When we approached the tram stop, near the place where my father was shot, we hear three shots go over the car. He stops the car and we crawl out and hit the pavement. It is only when I see him filming that I realize what is happening. It is the tram I missed. People are running out as if they are trying to escape from the devil, or a curse. I watch, but I can't comprehend what is happening. The scene reminds me of a sports match after the game when the fans run onto the field. But these today ran right to the enemy. The tram doors faced the snipers. Two victims—one a child. I watch, trying to understand, but can only say, Why? Why? Why?

We the citizens of Sarajevo are the craziest people in the world. We all know we can be killed at any moment, but we risk—test our destiny. Today, I could have been one of the killed or injured. It could have been anyone. We are all someone. We all belong to somebody.

We are human beings—only guilty because we exist. We all have somebody somewhere that loves us—even in your white, clean world or in this black Sarajevo.

People who shoot at the trams are not as evil as they seem. They do not want to kill us; they only want to cripple us.

As a witness to this, you would at least think I would scream as an animal, but NO!

I have no voice!

My mouth is shut! Silenced!

But my eyes watch and they will remember!

Nine days later, I receive a final fax:

Do not contact me again, I am leaving tomorrow. Thank you for everything. It is signed,

A refugee.

On Sept. 29, 1994, Selma boards a tram near the center of town at three in the afternoon. She is headed to the 760-meter tunnel, the escape route Bosnians have dug under the airport runway, connecting Sarajevo with the rest of Bosnia. (The tunnel is about four feet wide and five feet high. It was originally dug for moving troops, but now serves as an escape route for civilians, as well as a life-line for transporting food into Sarajevo.) On the tram, Selma by chance meets a woman who worked with her father before the war. The woman lives outside Sarajevo, on the other side of the tunnel, and is on her way home.

"Why do I meet her?" Selma wonders. "It makes me think there is some power—God, or something." The woman is going to the tunnel with her sister-in-law and mother-in-law. They tell Selma to stay with them.

"When we get to the entrance of the tunnel, located in a house, we wait in a room for several hours. We are stuck. It is so crowded. At first, I shift my weight from one foot to the other. But then, I lift one foot up and there is no room to put it back down. At the end of my wait, my feet aren't even touching the ground. Finally, we get to the next room. It is so damp, and it smells terrible. We start through the tunnel at about 10:40 in the evening. It only takes about twenty minutes, but it seems endless. We come out on the other side of the airport, and climb a small hill and are exposed to the enemy. They even shine lights on that area so people are more exposed. My dad's friend says, 'Hurry up and go straight!' We come out from the tunnel and become a target. There are snipers on the mountain above. Finally, we come to her house. It's about midnight. She makes her husband get up and start a fire. She gives me something to eat. Then they look at each other and tell me it is time to go. He guides me to Mount Igman and then climbs with me for two hours. I'll never forget that.

"There is a bus in that area, going toward Croatia, from Bosnia, but it is too dangerous to get on the bus at that point by the tunnel, so the bus driver takes the bus empty, to the point where the Serbs can no longer see. Passengers climb Mount Igman on foot until they get to that safer place, then they board the bus.

"I feel desperate, horrible about leaving Sarajevo. I am afraid I will be killed. I turn around. I want to go back to Sarajevo.

"It starts to rain, just enough to make everything muddy. I keep slipping and falling down. I grab hold of small trees, but end up with my face in the mud. From Igman, I can see Sarajevo. I feel so sad, so distant. I have never felt so alone. I want to go back. I feel something is breaking inside of me. I am so close to Sarajevo. I could turn and run across the airport, but they will kill me.

"Finally I come to the bus. I am completely covered with mud and very wet. My luggage is wet. I go behind the bus and change my clothes. My shoes are full of mud. My father's friend waits until the bus leaves. I could never have made it without him. On the mountain, how would I have known how far to climb? I will never forget him and his wife.

"As I wait for the bus to leave, I am so scared. I don't have papers to leave—only my bus ticket and my passport. (During the war, men and women of military age, eighteen years or older, were not allowed to leave Bosnia without special permission.) At each checkpoint soldiers ask to see everyone's papers. I see everyone has the necessary permission to leave Bosnia but me. I act stupid and show them the authorization to go through the tunnel. We left the tunnel miles back, but they don't say anything. My mother packed me some food, but I can't eat.

"Finally, at the Mostar checkpoint, a mixed military patrol, a policeman and a soldier get on the bus. The soldier says, 'Okay Selma, where is your permission to leave?' My heart is pounding. I look at him and shrug my shoulders. He looks at me and says, 'Oh, yeah, you are too young, you don't need it,' and closes my passport and gives it back to me. Then the policeman says, 'May I see that passport?' I am shaking. This is the last checkpoint. Are they going to pull me off the bus? Will they rape me? Kill me? They don't care who I am. I'm just a girl. The policeman looks at the date of my birth and says, 'You aren't that young.' He shuts my passport and gives it back to me. I don't know who he is—Croat or Muslim? In this moment I realized again, there is a power bigger than I am."

Cemetary

Memorial to children
Park-Downtown Sarajevo 1995

~ CHAPTER SEVEN ~
WAR CAKE

In war, time often seems to stand still, but it doesn't. People fall in love, marry, have babies, observe anniversaries and celebrate birthdays. During the siege of Sarajevo, many children celebrate four war birthdays. As in many parts of the world, the ritual of celebration, whatever the occasion, is not complete without a cake. In Bosnia during the war, it is called *ratni kolac* (pronounced kolach) or war cake.

While the Bosnian army, primarily men and a few women, holds the aggressor at bay on the front line, it is mostly the women left behind who assume total responsibility for the health and welfare of the children and many times, the elderly.

Women often assume the task of collecting humanitarian aid, sometimes standing in long lines in dangerous places or in the cold for hours. Many times mothers must decide whether to take their young children with them, or leave them at home alone. Staples such as oil, rice, beans, and flour are usually delivered in bulk to one building in each neighborhood, where it is distributed in a fairly organized manner, according to the number of members in each household. Everyone must supply his or her own paper or plastic bags for food and containers for the oil. Often deliveries are erratic, and the amount of aid received small. Rice and beans are frequently distributed, causing residents to ask, "Does the world think Sarajevo is a *third-world* country?" The resentment comes because Sarajevans feel the international community—especially Europe, is responding to the tragedy in Bosnia as though Bosnia is not a part of Europe.

Some families are lucky enough to have a small garden, lessening their dependence on humanitarian aid. During my first visit to the city in 1993, Jagger, Renata's brother-in-law, takes me to visit a family living across the river and up the side of the mountain from Renata's apartment. The father is in the army and stationed outside of Sarajevo. The mother cares for their two children, a girl ten, and a boy six. The day we visit, our host makes pita, a baked Bosnian pastry filled with savory fillings. On more than one occasion during the siege I eat empty pita, but because of their garden, she fills hers with fresh vegetables.

After lunch, the little girl takes me outside the two-room cottage to show me their garden etched into the cliff. The war's front line lay just over the ridge only several hundred meters away. The view of Sarajevo takes my breath away. My eyes focus on hundreds of red tile roofs, or at least what is left of them. From a distance, the devastation doesn't look so severe. The little girl stands at the edge of the cliff near several tomato plants loaded with ripe tomatoes. She sweeps her arm out declaring, "Paradise!" I first think, "Wow, she really loves Sarajevo." Then I think, "Yes! It is paradise, even in war!" Later, I learn the Bosnian word for tomato is *paradajz*, pronounced paradise. In any case, I will never forget the view, the tomatoes, or the hospitality that day.

Many women I meet, because of the uncertain and unfamiliar circumstances of war, try to comfort their children by recreating familiar tastes from the life they enjoyed before the war.

After the siege begins in the spring of 1992, days quickly stretch to weeks, weeks to months, and, finally, months to years. Ana, a mother of a nine-year-old boy, says, "The war turned washing, cleaning, cooking, and other ordinary day-to-day housework into a daily struggle for survival. We suddenly found ourselves in a situation we never dreamed possible—living without electricity, gas, water, and adequate food. But we discover a strange strength and power inside us. We feel abandoned by the rest of the world and left alone to die, but pure pride, spite, and anger forces us not to give up."

To create familiar, comforting food for her son, Ana experiments with substitutions and exchanges war recipes, some kept by older women since World War II. To make cream, she mixes yeast, powdered milk, water, and salt, and allows it to ferment overnight. For fake mayonnaise, she cooks flour and water, and then stirs in powdered milk and oil. Especially for her son, she makes French fries from corn flour, white flour, bicarbonate of soda, and a little water. After mixing all the ingredients, she rolls the mixture out with a rolling pin, cuts out shapes resembling French fries, and then bakes them. Often she picks nettles and makes soup by adding, rice, salt, and water. Her specialty is "paste," a substitute for chicken paste. She mixes two large spoons of dried breadcrumbs, two spoons of dried yeast (large bags of it are often found in humanitarian aid packages), one onion chopped and roasted, and enough water to bind the ingredients together, and then adds all the spices she has available, including mustard if she has it. Finally, she spreads the mixture on crackers or bread, and her family enjoys a hint of a treat they knew before the war.

If there is wood, carpet, old shoes, books, or parts of furniture to build a fire, Ana uses her family's flour ration to make bread. After preparing the dough, she uses her pressure cooker to save energy. She cooks the dough about ten minutes, opens it, turns it over, and then cooks the other side. She says, "When it is done the bread is heavy and dense, but it is hot and smells so good. In the winter, we cannot wait to eat it at dinner, so we eat it the moment it comes out of the pot."

When I go to Italy to buy supplies, I always bring back cinnamon and vanilla, almond, and lemon flavoring for women in the neighborhood. Some might think it a frivolous gift, but the tiny bottles are inexpensive and take no space in my pocket. The small gifts return the women to a tiny part of their pre-war reality of creating desserts with real flavoring. Women tell me sweets are a big part of Sarajevan culture. It is only after the war that I understand how important! When the stores reopen, I discover dessert shops scattered all over town, especially on every block of the main pedestrian cobblestone street of the old town.

Cake or kolac as it is called in Bosnian, tops the list of favorite desserts, especially ones made at home. A good host would not be caught without kolac to offer unexpected guests. Bosnians pride themselves on their hospitality, especially hospitality given to strangers. During the 1984 Olympics there were not enough hotel rooms in Sarajevo to accommodate visitors, so the government appealed to the people to open their homes to visitors, and they did.

Although cake improvised in war circumstances usually can outwardly be recognized as cake, many times it's difficult to identify the ingredients. Certainly, it won't contain eggs, and maybe not milk, flour, or flavoring. There is no shortage of flour. I arrived with several tons of it on my first flight into the city, but with the absence of electricity and gas, flour is useless unless you want to make dried pasta for a future meal or glue for a child's art project.

Bread or cracker crumbs top the list as the best flour substitute for war cake. Ana calls it "bread cake." She mixes a couple of cups of dried breadcrumbs with a little oil, sugar or artificial sweetener, a little powdered milk or water, and presses it into a cake pan. Before serving, she spreads the top with the cream mixture made from powdered milk and yeast.

On the birthday of a friend's four-year-old daughter, a teenage boy brings a gift—the cake. The children and the adults are surprised to find raisins in the cake, but the teenager says, "No, they are not real raisins; they are artificial. My mother made them from soy flour and concentrated juice." Everyone is amazed at how much the chewy dark brown pieces resemble raisins. Later he admits it is a joke. The raisins are real. Then someone comments, "It is sad, even tragic; we have gone without for so long we do not recognize reality even when we are eating it."

During my visits to Sarajevo in the siege, various hosts serve me war cake. Always, they place two pieces on the plate—I think a symbol of abundance and of generosity. If only one piece is available, they cut it in half to make two. I never question the custom or the ingredients. The taste is not important. What is important is the woman's hospitality and her effort to maintain a sense of normalcy and tradition for herself and for her family amid the chaos of war.

Celebrating milestones such as birthdays, weddings, and anniversaries affirms our existence and help us define who we are. For anyone caught in war—guest or host—kolac, however prepared, brings a sense of sanity and hope for the future.

Secondary Music School Sarajevo
Front: Vanja Ljiljak Back: Farida Musanović

~ CHAPTER EIGHT ~
REVOLT AGAINST DESTINY

Early in the war, on May 27, 1992, dozens of people are waiting for bread outside a bakery on Vaso Miskin Street, the pedestrian street leading into the Bascarsija, the old town. The aggressor on the mountain fires a shell, and it explodes near the bakery, mutilating and killing twenty-two civilians waiting in the bread line.

The following day, Vedran Smailović, a cellist with the Sarajevo Opera Company, comes to the bloodstained site with cello and chair in hand. Dressed in formal attire, he sits in full view of the mountain and plays Albinoni's *Adagio.* Risking his life, he returns there to play the same piece every day for twenty-two consecutive days. International journalists, moved by Smailović's response to the tragedy, transmit his picture around the world. It is one of the images that moved me to come to Sarajevo.

In his book, *My People,* Abba Eban, one of the founding fathers of the state of Israel and often referred to as a "peace dove," writes about artistic activities in the Warsaw Ghetto: "Whatever its ordeals to survival, the ghetto nevertheless supported a flourishing culture; artistic and intellectual activities seemed to burgeon as physical strength flagged. Theaters functioned to the end."

And, so it was in Sarajevo. Beginning with Vedran's musical memorial to those killed in the bread line, Sarajevo throughout the siege relies on art, music, theater, dance and the written word to resist the enemy and overcome despair.

In the summer of 1993, on my first day walking alone in Sarajevo, I see a young girl carrying a violin. This is war; I expect guns, not musical instruments. At various times in my life, I attempted to master the violin. Although I never did, it has always been my favorite instrument. I stop to say hello, but she does not speak English and I do not speak Bosnian.

To my surprise, a few days later our paths cross again when a friend invites me to a promotion of a new publication, *The Diary of Zlata Filipović,* printed then as a small booklet with the help of UNI-

CEF. (Viking Penguin Books later publishes the work, which documents a young girl's experience in the siege of Sarajevo, as *Zlata's Diary*. It eventually makes the *New York Times* best-seller list.)

That Saturday morning I arrive at the site of the promotion, the former basement restaurant Jez, now closed because of the war. There is a generator for the occasion, but the lighting is dim. As I make my way down the dark stairway, I enter Zlata's world—her family, school friends, and a former teacher. In the flickering light, a young girl reads from the small booklet *The Diary of Zlata Filipović:*

"Monday, June 29, 1992

Dear Mimmy,

BOREDOM! SHOOTING!!! SHELLS!!! PEOPLE BEING KILLED!!! DESPERATION!! STARVING!! MISERY!! TERROR!!! That is my life. The life of an innocent eleven year old school girl!"

And,

"Sunday, October 11, 1992

Dear Mimmy,

Today is a memorable day in our family. Today we brought a little stove in our flat, in the kitchen. Oh, it is so fine, so warm! Mum and Dad and I, we all had a nice bath. With collected rain water, still, but never mind. No water, no electricity yet!"

After several more readings from the diary, the teenage violinist I had met on the street earlier in the week plays a haunting, unfamiliar melody. I am glad for the darkness because I cannot stop my tears.

The program ends and our hosts offer us a drink of orange powder mixed with water and iodine purification tables. I sit lost in thought. These few moments have transported me to another time and place—to home and my teenage son, who has studied piano since the age of four, and now attends a performing arts high school. I force myself back to the present and climb the stairs to the glaring daylight and tuneless reality of war. In my hand, I clutch a half-sheet of paper with the printed text Zlata read at the end of the program: *"The message of Zlata Filipović ... From the coast of my peace, happiness ...ugly powers of war ... drag me away. I feel like a swimmer ... forced into cold water ... Why have they stolen my childhood? I was happy for every new day ... for the sun, play ... I did not need anything better. I have less and less strength to swim in this cold water. The only thing I want to say is: PEACE!"*

A few days later, I attend a concert, the first of many I will attend on every visit to Sarajevo. There is no charge. To standing room only, the Sarajevo String Quartet plays Boccherini, Haydn, and Schubert at the Kamerni Theater 55 in the center of town. Because there is no electricity, they perform in an outer room to take advantage of natural light (a room not facing the guns on the mountain). Again, the music transports me to a timeless space found only in our souls—a place no one can destroy—not even Chetniks on the hills around Sarajevo.

Andre Malraux, a minister in France under President Charles de Gaulle, once wrote, "Art is a revolt against destiny." Sarajevo's artists, young and old, beginners and professional, manifest this spirit throughout the war. I see ten-year-old frail ballet hopefuls arrive for ballet lessons on their bicycles, faint not from the fear of their journey through sniper territory, but from lack of food. When she can scavenge it, their ballet teacher distributes small food items, such as crackers or half-dollar-size tins of jam, the kind I take for granted in restaurants back home.

Many dancers and musicians in Sarajevo began their study at the Music School, an old Austrian-Hungarian building a short block behind the Catholic cathedral, one of Sarajevo's landmarks. The worn stone steps of the entrance spill out over the narrow sidewalk, almost onto the street. The building houses three separate divisions. On the first floor is the primary, Mladen Pozajić, (grades 1-8), on the second floor, the secondary, Srednja Muzicka, (grades 9-12) and on the third floor, the Academy (college level). Throughout the war, the sounds of strings, horns, drums, and badly out-of-tune pianos pour out of the broken windows. One day a shell hits the top floor, blasting a hole in the concert hall wall, but the students do not miss a note.

Farida Musanović, a piano teacher at the school, served as director of the secondary school for three years during the war. She told me, "The only way I could fight was to work at my school as hard as I could. That is why I was at the school every day during the summer of 1992, a time of severe shelling. When the war started it took me a while to realize it was war. We all thought it was just some mean boys wearing ski masks. We believe someone will stop them and we will live in peace like before. We believe the Yugoslav army will protect us, not attack us. We know the international community will defend us because we are not armed. We are sure they will not let us be hungry here in Europe. We are mistaken! Day after day, it is more difficult to live without water, electricity and food. I don't care if I am hungry, but to tell my daughters there is no food, that is hard. It is also hard when one of my friends, my daughter's English teacher, is killed in front of her house. It is even difficult to bury her because the aggressor shoots at funerals, so we had to bury her at night."

Often when in Sarajevo, I visit Farida during her lessons with her students. As in my son's piano teacher's studio, two grand pianos sit side by side—one for the student and one for her. Students struggle to remember notes and offer the same feeble excuses as to why they didn't practice, as students do back in the States. Sitting in her studio reminds me of the many hours I spent with my son at his lessons. Only one thing is different—the pianos in Sarajevo are badly out of tune. The discord moves me to solicit a tuning instrument from the Yamaha Piano Co., which I deliver to the school in 1996.

During the war, out-of-tune instruments were not the major hardship the students and teachers faced. Farida remembers freezing weather in January 1993. She says, "There was no heat, water or electricity in the music school. It was so cold my pen wouldn't write. One of my students, Vanja, cut the tips of her gloves off so she could still wear them while playing the piano. During that time, the Chambre Theatre produced *Hair*. I can't imagine how the performers managed because I know they were cold and hungry. But at the end of the performance, the audience cried. The production of *Hair* and Vanja's determination to practice were both a sort of fight—a fight against despair."

At home, Farida attempted to create a positive atmosphere. She said, "We often gathered with neighbors and shared what we had— coffee or war cakes. Once, my husband brought home two apples. We hadn't had apples for months. We shredded one, and shared it, then gave the other to a woman in our neighborhood with a baby. She and the baby's grandmother would go down to the Miljacka River at night to wash diapers, because in daytime it was too dangerous. What I dream of throughout the war, besides peace, is a long, warm shower."

When the war began in 1992, twelve-year-old Jasna is just beginning her piano study at the elementary music school. Actually, her family didn't own a piano, so her father walked with her every day to the music school so she could practice. Eventually the family found a piano and throughout the war, Jasna continued to learn to play as a way to survive. On October 24, 1995, I attend her primary school graduation recital. For some, war brings dreams and accomplishments to a halt, but Jasna, after three war years at the piano, emerges an accomplished pianist and a compassionate young woman.

Compassion for life moves artists to forget themselves and create. When I arrive in Sarajevo in the summer of 1993, American writer Susan Sontag is there directing Samuel Beckett's play *Waiting for Godot*. Sontag's son, the writer David Rieff, had visited the city early in the war and returned home and told his mother she really ought to go there. *Godot*, a play about two friends who wait for someone who never arrives, is a perfect choice for Sarajevans, who wait for water, electricity, humanitarian aid, and intervention from the international community. Actors performed by candlelight and played to packed audiences. Sontag gave herself to Sarajevo not only as an artist but also as a friend. She often acted as a link between people in Sarajevo and their family and friends outside the city. After the summer of 1993, Sontag returned to the city on numerous occasions, always bringing material or emotional support.

Bianca Jagger and the Irish rock group U2 also visit Sarajevo during the war to express their solidarity and bring aid.

Throughout the siege, local artists use their talents to overcome the pain and boredom of war. A large sculpture made from hundreds of pieces of broken glass sits in the lobby of Sarajevo's Art Academy. A group of visual artists called Trio Sarajevo produces a series of postcards depicting famous images such as Leonardo da Vinci's

Mona Lisa and Andy Warhol's red-and-white Campbell's Chicken Soup can. The trio redesigned the images and logos with a slant on the siege. *Mona Lisa* with a tear running down her face sits in the forefront of a picture of a destroyed Sarajevo. The Campbell's soup can is riddled with bullet holes and reads, Sarajevo's Condensed Chicken with Rice Soup. The back of each card reads, "This document has been printed in war circumstances. (No paper, no ink, no electricity, no water. Just good will.)"

Good will is important. The courage of these artists, dancers, actors, singers, writers, and musicians, both professionals and students, connects me to Sarajevo and makes me understand that art sustains life by giving it meaning. Even in the worst situations, these creators are able to revolt. They seize the moment and transform it into whatever they want it to be. In turn, those of us viewing the process are also transformed. Coming to Sarajevo, I had hoped to find a resistance movement, but never dreamed it would come in the form of art, ballet, music, theatre, and sculpture.

One of the final statements of resistance through art comes soon after the Dayton Peace Agreement is signed and the curtain falls on the siege of Sarajevo. After the Serbs pull the tanks away and locals return to the mountains, they find tens of thousands of spent mortar casings of all sizes—remnants of the shells Serbs fired on Sarajevo during the years of the siege. Metal artists in the old town set to work hammering swords into plowshares. Traditional designs and scenes of Sarajevo are etched into the metal, transforming instruments of war into objects of beauty and of peace.

Left: Linda Beekman
Sorting shoes for Sarajevo Ballet Company-National Theater
October 1994

~ CHAPTER NINE ~
A PRETEND PEACE

On October 22, 1994—thirty months into the siege, I travel to Sarajevo for the third time. My two wheeled bags bulge at the seams with $4,000 worth of donated dance supplies for the Sarajevo Ballet Company.

In early June, through an online report from the Associated Press, I learn that on May 28, twenty dancers from Sarajevo's pre-war ballet company of sixty performed their first production during the war to a packed audience in Sarajevo's National Theater. The AP report said the company decided to stage the ballet "to prove to themselves war could not stop them." It also said they chose Ravel's *Bolero* because the piece is traditionally danced barefoot and some of the dancers no longer had shoes.

Ballet has a long tradition in Sarajevo. Before the war, the company performed classical and modern pieces in repertoire. When the war started, many dancers left, especially those originally from other parts of Europe. The remaining male dancers joined the army to defend their country. Several male dancers missed *Bolero* performances because they still served on the front line.

When I read they had no shoes, I immediately know the focus of my next trip to Sarajevo will be dancewear for the company. I find a copy of *Dance Magazine*, and start calling the toll-free numbers of dance supply companies. Within ten days supplies begin arriving and continue arriving up until the day before I leave for Sarajevo. No one turns me down.

Now, as Renata and I open the bags of supplies in her living room she is stunned. She says, "No one has thought about us like this in this war." We set to work sorting tights, leotards, dance skirts, leg warmers, and makeup, making packages for each of the dancers, while attempting to choose the right size and color for each person. The following day we walk about a quarter of a mile along the river to the stage door of the theater, each of us pulling a bag. As we climb the stairs the music of *Bolero* gets louder, but as we enter the large practice room it abruptly stops. We are expected! There are greetings, introductions, and excitement on their part and mine. As I sit on the floor searching through dozens of pairs of ballet and toe shoes for the correct sizes for each dancer, I feel a bit like Santa Claus. As always in the siege, the contents of the package aren't nearly as important as the knowledge that people halfway around the world care.

It is good to lift the dancer's spirits by bringing them the tools they need for their art. In turn, they will lift the spirits of those around them. On the opening night of *Bolero*, the AP reporter quotes a member of the audience who said, "I have the feeling that I'm away from the harsh reality of my everyday life. If nothing else, the music, the dancers, and the atmosphere make me drift away to another world."

Unfortunately, *Bolero* is not scheduled for performance during my time in Sarajevo. *Bolero* has never been my favorite piece of music, but as I watch the company rehearse, I realize it is an appropriate choice not only because of the fact the piece is danced barefoot. The repetitive droning, and the dancers' constant circular movement—around and around, on and on, again and again—this never-wavering persistence captures the drudgery of the siege and their determination to survive it. Of course, the music finally ends, but will the siege?

When I arrive in Sarajevo on this trip, I realize things are a little better when I find a real taxi to take me to Renata's apartment for only fifteen dollars! In the spring of this year, the international community brokered a cease-fire. For the most part shelling has ceased, except for the times the aggressor decides to shell, and there is still no freedom of movement in or out of the city—a measure of true freedom anywhere. I am naïve. Because of the cease-fire I anticipate real peace conditions, but nothing has changed—only a city increasingly desperate and the craziness derived from attempting to live a reality that doesn't exist.

The siege has not ended, but people behave as if it has. The trams run—at least on the days the Serbs don't shoot at them. Some official made the premature decision to remove the Pink Floyd concrete slab protecting pedestrians from snipers near the center of town. Everywhere, residents are replacing the UNHCR plastic, used to cover broken windows, with glass. It's fall, but amid this busy optimism Sarajevans are preparing community gardens for spring—a sure sign they expect food shortages to continue.

In spite of seemingly positive activity, the city is gray and lifeless. Discouragement lingers like a morning fog. Young people sit in cafes, drinking Turkish coffee and smoking cigarettes, waiting—killing time until they can begin their lives again.

I hear shooting in the distance. Every time I return to Sarajevo I feel more afraid. I am frustrated with everyone, including myself. How can the international community declare there is peace here when Serbs and their guns still sit on the mountains above the city? Where is local resistance? Why don't Sarajevans do something, anything, but sit and drink coffee and smoke cigarettes? Or maybe this is the resistance—to act as if all is well? Sometimes I think it was better when people had to hide in basements. At least then there were no illusions. Sarajevo is still a prison. I take solace in my journal:

The aggressor on the mountains—the crazies as they are called surround the city. Are they monsters with dark wild beards—cutthroats who have lost their humanity? Or are they someone's loving child, parent or spouse? Whoever they are, they continue to kill and maim unarmed citizens. Yesterday seven people in a trolley—shot down all at once, like sitting ducks at a carnival game. Today, twelve people wounded—a shell—a grenade as they say, has shattered flesh and bones and lives. Children without arms and legs will never touch, run, or dance. Torture is forbidden in our civilized world. Yet this city, on the continent of Europe, an overnight train from Vienna, remains captive—a concentration camp. Like the Warsaw Ghetto, it struggles to keep its sanity through the familiar, through tradition and the arts. But in the end will the walls here collapse like those in Berlin? Or will the inhabitants, like those at Babi Yar, fall dead into a black hole, while the United Nations and the world monitors their passing?

(At Babi Yar, near Kiev in Ukraine, Nazis killed 33,771 men, women, and children in a large pit on Sept. 29 and 30, 1941. In November 1995, the wall of guns surrounding Sarajevo fall, but only after Serbs attack the U.N.-protected "safe haven" of Srebrenica, creating the worst massacre in Europe since World War II. There, in July 1995, Serbs slaughter more than 7,000 men, teenage boys, and other victims, and then bury them in mass graves.)

One morning, Renata and I walk one hour to Alipasino Polje to visit her baby, who is spending a few days with his grandmother. Returning home, I see a large vase of flowers sitting on the curb. Renata explains the flowers are in memory of a six-year-old girl killed not by a sniper's bullet or a mortar shell, but by a U.N. tank. The driver, going too fast, drove up onto the curb and hit a tall metal streetlight, which in turn fell onto the small child. In that instant, a life protected by the U.N. Protection Force was lost.

Distraught at this child's death and the continuation of the siege, I ask myself, "Who am I to come to Sarajevo—an ordinary person unable to do anything about this tragedy?" For the dancers I bring sixty pairs of toe shoes—pink satin, shiny, and clean. If twelve dancers have twenty-four feet and one sniper shoots or one shell falls, how many feet will still dance? When I first came to Bosnia, I thought I was a pacifist. I tried not to take sides. Now I say, "Bring on the air strikes! There is no honor in being neutral in an unjust situation." I feel helpless; I have no energy left for this. I will go to Italy and buy food for those in my neighborhood here, bring it back, and then leave Sarajevo and never return.

The following day, I hitch a ride to the airport and catch a transport plane to Ancona. I climb through the tail carrying my empty bag and backpack. I also carry an accumulation of grief, pain, and frustration—almost more than I can bear. In less than an hour I arrive in Italy. From the airport, I walk to the little village of Castelferretti to catch the bus to Ancona to shop. Plum and apple trees line the streets, climbing roses cling to wrought-iron fences, and red geraniums grace each balcony, as only they can in Italy. The air is clean, the buildings intact, and the shops overflow with every kind of food. I question my perception. Did I just arrive from a war zone?

But I am filthy and disheveled; the smell of burned garbage lingers in my hair and clothes, and on my luggage, confirming reality—yes, I have just arrived from Sarajevo. I fight back the tears. Part of me does not want to continue returning to Bosnia, but I will. At some point during the last sixteen months, I have made a commitment to the people of Sarajevo to see the tragedy of the siege to its end.

This is my second side trip to Italy during these three weeks in Sarajevo. Before, one could fly out and back to Sarajevo in the same day, but the new rule states no flying in and out on the same day. But staying overnight is okay. It allows me to shop in a better grocery store in Ancona, and permits me an evening in my hotel room to strip all the excess cardboard and wrapping from my purchases— fitting as much as possible in my backpack and in my coat pockets. Various people in Renata's neighborhood have added items to my shopping list—batteries, contact lens wash, bicycle tire repair kit, coffee, sugar, butter, raisins, honey, vanilla flavoring. Shopping is frustrating because I want to take the whole store with me, especially the large sausages and slabs of cheese. My friends in Sarajevo have also given me letters to mail—to France, Germany, England, Austria, United States, Sweden, Croatia, and Australia.

Some of the supplies I buy will go to Irma and her parents and younger sister. Selma is gone now. It's almost a month since she escaped through the tunnel and made her way to Split. A good friend of her parents works in Split and agreed to house her until her future is determined.

I return to Sarajevo and deliver the supplies. In several days I am back at the airport, ready to depart Sarajevo and begin my journey back to Florida. I arrive early and stand outside, writing in my journal. I feel lucky to have spent another three weeks in the city without harm. I casually look up and gasp. Across the makeshift parking lot, Ukrainian soldiers carry one not so lucky—a comrade concealed in a brown-stained wooden box. The procession winds through the mud and comes to a halt. The casket is placed on a long, narrow rickety table, and draped with the blue U.N. flag. About one hundred soldiers, men and women, form two rows to stand guard beside their

fallen friend until the transport arrives. Who will welcome this trav-
eler home—mother, father, son, daughter, lover, husband, or wife?
The plane arrives and the cargo loaded. This soul, the latest casualty
of the war in Bosnia, departs Sarajevo.

Soon my plane arrives, but this time I go to Split, not Ancona. I
spend a day and a night along the coast of the Adriatic with Selma.
We eat in a small restaurant in the neighborhood. The last time we
ate together was with her family in Sarajevo last February. Then
we ate only empty pita. Now, we eat fresh fish, potatoes, and salad.
It's difficult to understand how Sarajevo can be so close yet so far
away. She waits now for her family to decide if they will escape
from Sarajevo too.

The following evening, in pouring rain, Selma and I take the bus
to the port in Split, where I board an overnight ferry to Ancona.
We say goodbye and agree the next time we meet will be in the
United States.

I go straight to my stateroom and fall into bed. Sarajevo has
drained me. I feel safe locked in my cubicle. I have again escaped
the siege unharmed, but what about the friends there I again leave
behind? Will it ever end?

Downtown Sarajevo

Downtown Sarajevo

~ CHAPTER TEN ~
MARCH 1995

After waiting four days in Ancona for the airport in Sarajevo to reopen, I feel lucky to be in Sarajevo again. It's March 1995, and this is my fourth trip to Bosnia from the United States. A blanket of clean, moist snow covers the city, causing it to look more like a set for the *Nutcracker ballet* than a war zone.

Once inside Renata's apartment, the illusion vanishes. The cold and dark confirm not much has changed since my visit here last fall. Electricity and gas still arrive sporadically. At least now fresh food trickles into the city daily through the 760-meter tunnel Bosnians dug under the airport connecting Sarajevo to the rest of Bosnia. The tunnel is little more than a narrow one-way footpath, not even high enough for most adults to stand up. But like a tube connecting a breathless patient to a respirator, it allows the city to breathe, permitting some to escape and others to return. Last fall, Selma left through the tunnel. Early this year her sister Irma, her parents and little sister followed. Recently the whole family arrived in the United States.

Thanks to the tunnel, for the first time in three years, oranges, bananas, potatoes, and garlic are available in the markets, and cheese and sausages in shops, although all at extremely high prices. In my money belt, under six layers of clothing, is several hundred dollars to buy food for the children of the Mjedenica School, a school for children with learning difficulties. I first visited the school with the Beati group in August 1993. On that day, in the tiny yard next to the entrance to the building, we found a teenage boy tending a small vegetable garden. Several younger boys were playing soccer in the narrow, dusty street in front of the building.

During a meeting with the director that day, she told us the school was founded in 1946. Before the war, about 120 students attended the school as day students or boarded at the school weekdays, returning to their families on weekends. In April 1992, when barricades went up cutting Sarajevo off from the world, about forty-five students, ages seven to twenty, could not return to their homes only a few kilometers away. Parents could not travel to Sarajevo to take their children home. Responsibility for the children's care fell on the teachers, who soon organized twenty-four-hour work-shifts instead of the usual eight. Many teachers also had children of their own to care for at home.

The first winter of the war, teachers and students lived together in one room; the only room with a wood-burning stove. Teachers burned doors as fuel. Huddled together on mattresses on the floor, the children drank warm powdered milk, flavored with cocoa when available. One teacher who worked at the school for twenty-three years said, "Before the war we were a school. In the war, we have become a family."

The building is built into the side of a hill and contains dorms, numerous classrooms, and a gym. In 1993, the gym became open-air when a mortar knocked a large hole in the wall. In an impressive wood and metal workshop, students make wooden toys, model houses, wire spiders, and other metal creatures. Throughout the school, the children's artwork is displayed on the walls, but their work does not reflect the violence of the war, only sweet animals, flowers, and butterflies. Even in war, potted philodendrons grow in every windowsill.

At the end of the meeting with the director that summer day, she holds up half a bottle of alcohol and a few Band-Aids, saying, "This is our first-aid kit—all the medical supplies we have left for all these children." I immediately rummage through my backpack and pull out some alcohol wipes and Band-Aids, thinking, "Now I understand the meaning of the expression Band-Aid fix." The meeting ends abruptly when a civil defense siren sounds, and shells began to explode nearby. The director quickly runs outside to the street to gather the playing children.

Since that visit I have often thought of the children and wanted to do something for them. Now, more than a year-and-a-half later I return to the school. Everything looks the same, except the little garden by the entrance is enclosed in a makeshift greenhouse made from UNHCR-donated plastic. A new director, a man, and some older students are in the courtyard chopping wood. Some students are now back home with their parents. The ones remaining are back in their dorms and classrooms, but there still isn't much heat, so everyone wears a coat and hat inside the building.

With Irma now in the States, I ask her best friend to help me haul my bags up the hill to the school. Through the generosity of many people back home, I have brought underwear, socks, crayons, color markers, hair ribbons, shampoo, soap, alcohol wipes, lots of Band-Aids, and other practical supplies, all collected specifically for these children. Large blocks of cheese and several pounds of sausage protrude from my backpack. A staff member helps me unpack and meticulously records each item I have brought into a ledger book. Later in the day, another staff member drives me down the icy hill to a market in the old town to buy several crates of bananas, oranges, potatoes, garlic, and onions.

A few days later, when I return to the school, I am delighted to find two banana peels on the snowy sidewalk in front of the build-ing. Already thinking ahead, I ask the director how I can help them the next time I come to Sarajevo. He hesitates, and I brace myself for some impossible request. Then he says, "What we really need are plastic cups and soup spoons." Astonished he would ask for some-thing so simple I rush off the next day, with Irma's friend, to a flea market to buy several dozen plastic cups and soup spoons.

Later that day, I deliver the cups and spoons to the school and say a final goodbye. On the way out, two teenagers are at work in the little greenhouse in front of the building. They proudly lift the plastic for me to peek inside. Row after row of tiny bright green lettuce plants reach for the warmth of the sun. Through these plants, I see Sarajevo's yearning for spring, a few green vegetables, and an ordi-nary simple life void of war.

In the evening I meet Alma, a friend I have known since I first came to Sarajevo in 1993. She is a thoughtful woman in her late twenties. Thick dark brown hair frames her warm brown, dreamy eyes and calm smile. She is small-framed but gently strong, both physically and mentally. Alma is optimistic, but deeply suffers the injustice of the siege. We go to a cafe, a normal event in most cities of the world, but this is a first for me since coming to Sarajevo. Until now, most stores, restaurants, and cafes have been closed. The place is packed, the music loud, and the cigarette smoke thick. Everyone is anxious to behave as though the war is over, but it is not. People act as though they are free, but they are not. Until the guns are removed from the mountains above the city and there is free movement in and out of the city, the war is not over.

It is just as cold inside the cafe as outside. There is no heat. I order hot chocolate. When it comes, I take one drink and gag. The taste and smell of boiled powdered milk reminds me of baby formula. Maybe it is. Someone bumps our table. The hot chocolate coats my pants—the only clothes I have because there was no room for anything in my luggage except supplies. We decide to leave; I am glad. I hate this pretend cafe and this pretend peace. What was once a fiery emotional resistance to the enemy has disintegrated into a desperate desire to return to normal life at any cost.

The following evening we try again, this time at Ragusa, a friendly, wood-paneled restaurant reminiscent of an English pub. The limited menu offers cheese, potatoes, and beer, all for a few German marks. Not bad considering a year earlier no restaurants were open. Alma and I share a plate of cold potatoes and a beer. We discuss her favorite author, Anais Nin. We talk about feminism and our dreams for our future—how to balance a relationship, family, and children, and not lose ourselves. Alma likes to dream and to make goals for her life. For now, until the war ends, dreaming is all she has.

Since early in the war, Alma has worked in a tiny bookstore—literally a hole in the wall. She receives no pay for her work and has few customers, but it gives her a reason to get up and out in the morning. She speaks fluent English, learned in school and polished during several summers spent in New York City as a tourist. Often she expresses fondness for the United States. But with the current lack of American government support in confronting nationalistic Serb aggression, she feels America has abandoned Bosnia. In May 1993, she expressed her feelings in a letter to a former boyfriend living in New York:

Dear Richard,

A little while ago, I searched in the darkness of the other room for my diary. Today there is no electric, water, gas or bread. As I write to you by candlelight, I am listening to the song, Soldier of Fortune, but I would rather call it Civilian of Fortune. I sit here, remembering the massacre in Vase Miskina Street last May, when 22 people died from a single explosion. You sit in the safe lap of the USA. The war in Bosnia hasn't touched you, but I hope that you will try to understand our situation here.

During this wartime, I have learned so many words of military terminology by translating some texts and by listening to the news in English. "Shell" or "heavy projectile," these words do not sound so horrifying in English as in the Bosnian language. I don't think a person even thinks about these words at all until one personally experiences their impact.

Richard, do you know what the word "shell" means in this war? It is not the shell you pick up on the beach, beside the ocean on a sunny day. Here the word shell means the mutilation of ordinary citizens. It's as if a monstrous beast with enormous teeth chewed off body parts, then spat out the bloody remains to litter the street. Large and small fragments of heavy projectiles slice into all parts of the human body: into the eyes, brain, limbs, stomach, and heart.

A heavy projectile falls with a terrible noise. It looks and feels as if a whole mountain has fallen into your house or street or onto you. Ninety percent of those who survive an explosion will be disabled; children, who will never run, touch or see again. It means that in an instant the person you love who is standing next to you disappears forever. Mothers and fathers are left without their children and children left without their parents. It means that in that split second, you lose everything, your past, present and future. It means blood, tears, and the big question 'Why?'

It's now morning in New York. I remember when I was

*there, we used to go to the Irish pub called Spinning Wheel. I re-
member how we would walk and laugh.*

  *Today, as every day, dust covers Sarajevo. Richard, in the
moment it takes for you to lift your glass to drink, hundreds will
die or be wounded here. In the moment it takes to say hello to your
friends, women will be raped and inmates in concentration camps
will be tortured and mutilated. We cannot understand all this—
We ask WHY? WHY? WHY?*

In late December 1993, after I returned home from my first
summer in Sarajevo, Alma wrote to me:

  *I still struggle to survive and hope I endure. We still do not
have enough water or food. We get electricity every fourth day and gas
sometimes every night. Every day many people get killed or wounded.
The shells keep falling. The horror goes on.*

  *I still work in the bookstore without pay, electricity or heat. I
look like a bear because I wear two sweaters, two pairs of stockings,
etc. and gloves and a hat. I hope we will meet again. I always remember you as a warm, good, and wise person ...*

I visit Alma's fifth-floor walk-up apartment three times during the
siege. One room of the apartment faces the mountain, in full view of
snipers, so it is not used. Alma, her brother, and their mother share
the back room.

Each time I visit, Alma's mother makes fried Bosnian doughnuts
from flour, water, and oil. Each time, I politely eat one and then
claim to be full. Although they are heavy and full of grease, they taste
good and fill the stomach, but I know Alma, her brother, and mother
depend on these doughnuts to survive. On every visit, her mother
cries and repeats the same story. She is retired. Before the war, she
received a pension, but now a large bag of flour has replaced her
monthly check. Alma's mother is diabetic and requires a balanced
diet. Flour is not enough. On one trip to Ancona, Alma asks me to
buy medicine for her mother.

Elderly people suffer a lot in this war. In addition to lack of
material needs, many like Alma's mother have lost everything they
worked for their entire life. They feel they are too old to have a fu-

ture, too old to start over.

This stay in Sarajevo is short, only ten days. Last fall I went back to college and now I am on spring break. The night before I leave the city, Renata invites some friends over. It's my birthday. The beer factory is working now, but empty bottles are scarce and must be returned for recycling immediately after use. We share beer and eat cheese and bread and *ratni kolac*—war cake, for my birthday.

The war seems to be winding down, but no one here really knows what is coming. Everyone is waiting for the end, or is it the beginning? After three years, Sarajevo is still waiting for the Serbs to remove their weapons from the mountains.

Early the next morning I leave the apartment before Renata is awake. I plan to return in September. As I leave, I don't realize Renata and the baby will be gone the next time I visit the city. Also, my next trip to Sarajevo will be the last I make under the siege. Next November, a lasting peace agreement is negotiated and initially signed. At long last, the guns on the mountains around Sarajevo are soon to be silenced and then, finally withdrawn.

*Mjedenica School
1992
Photo: Mjedenica
School*

*Mjedenica School
1992
Photo: Mjedenica
School*

*Mjedenica School 1995
Photo: Linda Beekman*

~ CHAPTER ELEVEN ~
FALL 1995

On August 28, 1995, for the second time in the war, the aggressor shells the open-air marketplace in Sarajevo, killing forty-one civilians and wounding eighty-five. On that day Renata is waiting for her husband to return home, so they can go shopping there. Just before he arrives home, she hears the explosion. It is the last straw; she cannot tolerate war any longer. She becomes determined to leave Sarajevo. She sends a fax to me in Florida, asking me to find her a scholarship at a dance school in the States, which will make it easier for her to get permission from her government to leave Sarajevo. After several calls to New York City, I fax her the offer she needs.

About a week later, with her two-year-old son in her arms, Renata flees Sarajevo through the tunnel under the airport runway. Once out on the other side, she begins her climb over Mount Igman. Explosions flash in the distance. She doesn't realize the attack on the marketplace was also the last straw for the international community. At long last, NATO is hitting Serb strongholds around Sarajevo with air strikes. Renata is leaving on the last day of the war!

Fear grips her throughout the night. She says, "I lived in fear and hardship for three and a half years during the war—always looking for food and water and wondering how long it will be before they kill me. At least my leaving was only one night. As I climbed in the darkness, I didn't know where I was or if there were land mines. Before the war, I often came to the mountain for picnics. But climbing in the dark, I didn't know if I was on the Bosnian or Serbian side. I was afraid we might die, but I was more afraid of what would happen to my baby if I died, leaving him alone on the mountain."

Often I have thought about how Renata survived the war and her journey over Mount Igman. Although during the war she questioned the presence of God on many occasions, once, when I asked her how she endured she quickly answered, "I don't know; I think God looks down upon me."

Several days after leaving Sarajevo, Renata and her two-year-old son arrive in Split, Croatia. She rents a small motel room in Podstrana, a strip of Adriatic Coast near Split, where she and the baby wait until U.S. Immigration permits them to enter the United States and join her parents in Florida. Formerly a tourist site, during the war Split and the surrounding area are inundated with thousands of refugees.

In the second week of September, I leave Florida and head to Bosnia for the fifth time. I arrive in Split on the overnight ferry from Ancona, weighted down with one wheeled bag filled with dental instruments and the other bag containing a violin, horn, and various supplies for the music school. Last spring, as I left Sarajevo, a dentist told me they regularly pull children's permanent teeth because they don't have filling compounds. Once home, I contacted a local dental supply salesman in Florida, who donated dozens of repossessed dental instruments. Kerr Dental Co. donated hundreds of capsules of filling compound. The supplies are for the children's dental clinic in Sarajevo.

Now, with the NATO strikes and Renata's long-awaited escape from Sarajevo, I sense, even before leaving home, a shift and uncertainty as to how to continue helping in Bosnia. The Serbs are gradually complying with orders to remove their artillery surrounding Sarajevo. It seems the air strikes prove what Sarajevans claimed all along—Serb guns could only be removed by force. At last, roads into the city are opening up, maybe a real sign the siege is ending.

I get off the overnight ferry from Ancona and grab a taxi to Podstrana. It's not difficult to find Renata. It's a small area and everyone knows everyone. Her room is on the water and contains a stove and small refrigerator. The Adriatic Sea is calm and clear as light blue glass. I hope the gentle sound of the water acts as a natural tranquilizer, healing her frayed nerves. In her last months in Sarajevo, I was able to reach Renata several times by phone. On one occasion she abruptly ends the conversation screaming, "I have to go; they are shelling again. I must get Haris away from the window."

Now the difficult part for Renata is living in limbo. It will take months for immigration services to process her file. Having responsibility for a two-year-old, full-time in tight quarters, demands much, but she has the energy of youth and seems resilient. In spite of having little means, she has managed to find a set of colored pencils. Sketches of the surrounding hills and sea hang on the bare walls of her one room refuge. On the table, an old jar she has decorated with shells and sea glass serves as a vase for wildflowers.

My dream since I first met Renata has been to see her outside Sarajevo, but this seems anti-climactic. I wanted her out during the war. In any case, I am thankful she is here now and grateful to the members of the St. Petersburg Quaker Meeting and many others who donated money to help her and her son during their time here as refugees. Her parents also have sent money to her and the grandson they have not yet met.

For twelve dollars a night, I find a room in a motel next door to Renata's place. It opens out to a small landing on the water. I hope the sea revives me, too. Renata and I share a simple meal and I go to bed early. The next day I must go to the U.N. Press Office to get a press card, so I can fly on the airlift. I have much to do on this trip besides visiting Renata. I have dental and music supplies and money to deliver to Sarajevo. Later in the month, I must travel to Zagreb to facilitate the arrival of volunteers for a friend's project. And I plan to visit Tuzla, a Bosnian city north of Sarajevo, to attend the Helsinki Citizens Conference, a gathering of citizens from all over the world, including Serbia, who want to work for peace.

I am not surprised when the U.N. Press Office refuses to issue me another press card. After two years, they finally realize I am not a journalist. I am grateful to have had entry to Sarajevo via the airlift for these past two years. I could have done nothing without a press card. But now I must travel the overnight bus trip to Zagreb to apply for an UNHCR card, which will permit me to travel on U.N. planes. An American operating a small project in Sarajevo asked me to transport money for him from the States, and to meet volunteers for his project when they arrive in Zagreb. In return, he agreed to request the UNHCR office in Zagreb to issue me a card identifying me as a volunteer for his project. I leave the heavy suitcase with the dental equipment with Renata in Split for a few days, and I catch a bus for the grueling twelve-hour trip to Zagreb.

When I arrive in Zagreb, I ask a woman at the bus station ticket counter if she can recommend a cheap place to stay. She says she has a nice room for rent in her home and if I wait a half-hour for her to get off work, she will take me there. We drive what seems to be forever, but finally arrive at her house. The tiny room on the third floor is spotless. A single bed with crisp white sheets waits for me for about fifteen dollars. I am amazed at the trust I have just put in a total stranger. There is no way but to follow my heart and intuition. Later, I find about eight to ten Bosnian refugees also living in the house. When I tell them I am on my way to Sarajevo, several people ask me to take letters to their family members there. One man is going into town near UNHCR and offers to show me the way. Within an hour of arriving there, I leave with my UNHCR Blue Operational Assessment Staff ID card. I am grateful for the card, a cargo plane ticket to Sarajevo once again. The following day I catch a huge cargo plane from the Zagreb airport, carrying troops and chain-link fencing. I arrive in Sarajevo about an hour later and hitch a ride downtown.

The city is depressingly dirty. When I see people carrying water jugs, my heart sinks—not much has changed. Each time I come here, I expect the situation to be better. It is difficult after more than two years to see people still carting water.

Tonight I spend the night alone in Renata's apartment; it feels so strange with her and the baby gone. Her husband is still in Sarajevo on army duty. Jagger has vanished to Italy. Although heavy artillery fire has subsided, I still hear sniper fire and am more afraid than in earlier visits. I have a sick feeling in my stomach; maybe my luck will run out. But this city, so dirty, so dangerous, and so depressing, continues to feel so familiar—as if I have never left. I unpack and take to the street to deliver the many letters I have brought for Sarajevans from their friends and family in the United States and Zagreb. I know my way in the dark, avoiding the uneven pavement and sidewalks damaged by explosions—pockmarks extending outward in perfect circles. Sarajevans call them roses and eventually fill them in with red tinted cement as a memorial to the people who died on those sites. When wet, the red cement looks like spilled blood.

I deliver the musical instruments and supplies to the music school. I know in a few weeks I will return to Zagreb, so I ask if there are any music supplies I can get for them. The answer is small music notation books; I make a note in my journal.

With telephone service now repaired, I call my friend Alma to ask if she will act as translator for me tomorrow at the paraplegic clinic when I visit Mirza, a fourteen-year-old boy from Dobrinja, a suburb near the airport. An old friend of Renata's who is a doctor at the paraplegic clinic told me about Mirza and asked if I could do something for him.

Seven months ago on February 26, 1995, while Mirza and his twelve-year-old sister stood near an armored tank in their neighborhood talking to French U.N. soldiers, a Serbian sniper held him in the scope of his rifle. Adults in the neighborhood had warned Mirza and his sister and other children about crossing the vulnerable main street to talk to the soldiers, but the temptation was too great—the soldiers gave the children candy. Suddenly, the sniper's bullet tore through Mirza's side, ricocheted through his lung and stomach and finally lodged in his spine. He said he was stunned and confused and didn't immediately realize what had happened. He first looked up at his sister, but then down at his clothes, absorbing his warm blood like a sponge. The French soldiers saved his life that day, but Mirza will never walk again. Since he was shot, he has endured seven operations and months of lying only on his side.

Alma and I walk up the steep hill to the paraplegic clinic at Kosevo Hospital. We each carry a small bag. We have apples and some oranges, a copy of Robinson Crusoe in English, several pairs of sweatpants, and some art supplies. Mirza is small for his age and is pale and depressed, but seems to be happy to have visitors. He speaks a little English and tells us, "Before I was shot, I used to lift weights and play tennis and soccer. Now I am a little mouse." Alma and I are at a loss at how to console him. What do you say to a fourteen-year-old who says he doesn't want to have his next birthday? Alma has seen much in Sarajevo during the siege but cannot come to terms with how a human being could deliberately shoot a child; and neither can I. Perhaps this is why early in the siege, Sarajevans stopped thinking of those on the mountains as human beings, but only as monsters or beasts. I have to agree. As Alma and I say good-bye to Mirza, we promise we will visit him again soon.

I fly back to Split and return to my room on the Adriatic coast. With Renata's help, I find a vehicle going to Tuzla, where I attend a grass-roots conference of the Helsinki Citizens Assembly. In July, Bosnian Serbs overran Dutch U.N. peacekeepers protecting the U.N.-safe haven of Srebrenica. With the Dutch soldiers looking on, the Serbs separated more than 7,000 men and older boys from the women and children. Later the men and boys are found in mass graves. The women and children flee over the mountains to Tuzla, creating a humanitarian crisis in the city.

The Helsinki conference is a gathering of many individuals and groups who want to influence a peaceful answer to the conflict in the former Yugoslavia. Susan Sontag attends, along with many other internationals. Serb peace activists from Belgrade travel four days to reach Tuzla, a journey usually taking several hours.

The trip from Split to Tuzla takes all day. I travel in a four-wheel-drive vehicle of Scottish Direct Aid, a humanitarian aid organization operating in Tuzla. We are five, two internationals from the organization, their driver from Tuzla, me, and a teenage girl from Tuzla returning after receiving medical aid in Spain. We drive through village after village—hundreds of charred homes reminding me of the images of the ruins by the Sarajevo airport, burned into my memory the day I first flew into Sarajevo.

Since my original trip to Bosnia in 1993, this is the first time I have traveled by car and see firsthand the efficiency of Serb "ethnic cleansing." People in the United States might think, "Those Balkan people have been fighting for hundreds of years; genocide could never happen in America." But it did. In 1838 to 1839, on "The Trail of Tears," the U.S. government removed more than 15,000 Cherokee

Indians from their homes in Georgia, North Carolina, and Tennessee, forcing them to walk to Oklahoma; 4,000 died. Those who made it were confined to camps, and their children sent to white boarding schools in an attempt to erase their native culture.

We arrive in Tuzla late in the evening. The driver's family lives in Tuzla and they offer me shelter in their apartment. I gladly accept. His parents are mixed—Serb and Muslim. His high school-age sister, along with an aunt who lost her home and family in the tragedy of Srebrenica, also live in the apartment. Tuzla was never under siege but suffered its own losses. On May 25, 1995, Bosnian Serbs fired a huge shell into a main street where dozens of young people, Muslim, Catholic, and Orthodox, sat in an outdoor cafe. In an instant, the community lost seventy-one members, most between seventeen and thirty years old. Now, they are buried side by side in a park. The teenage girl traveling in the car today was at the cafe that day. She was evacuated to Spain for plastic surgery to repair a shrapnel gash on her face. The scar remains.

The first day of the conference, we have a choice of several places to visit. I choose the bus going to three refugee collection sites. Except for refugees in the Hotel Europa in Sarajevo, most people I met during the siege enjoyed the privilege of living in their original home or at least part of it; at worst, they lived in a borrowed apartment. Now, coupled with the sights I saw on the road to Tuzla, for the first time since I coming to Bosnia, I begin to comprehend the magnitude of ethnic cleansing.

The first collection center is located in a school. A sea of refugees, mostly children, surrounds us; we drown in the crowd and the noise. Several of us have cameras and ask if we can take pictures. The children are quick to line up and the adults encourage it, anxious for any documentation of their situation to leak back to civilization. I am at a loss. I have seen much destruction in Sarajevo, but never so many homeless women and children.

After about a half-hour, we move on to another camp a few miles away. It's early October and cold. Here, refugees live in huts made from wooden frames covered with UNHCR plastic. The bunk beds are close together and remind me of scenes of concentration camps I have seen in pictures and movies. One teenage girl wearing only a lightweight sweater and sandals trails alongside me repeating *"Zima! Zima!"* (Cold! Cold!") (*Zima* also means winter in Bosnian.)

I am totally caught off guard. I didn't know I would see children today. In my suitcase I have dozens of small gifts for kids, but nothing with me. I do have some German money in twenty and fifty-mark notes. I decide to distribute what I can to women with babies or young children. As I quietly shake their hands, I discreetly press a folded note into their palms. I feel totally inept and helpless. This money is a drop in the bucket compared to their needs. I've been in and out of Sarajevo now for more than two years, but now I see another dimension of Serb aggression and understand more fully the extent of the violence and suffering in this war. I again feel angry and helpless. I am reminded of the poem thirteen-year-old Irma wrote when Sarajevo was first attacked in 1993:

You cowards,
One day you will gather to make agreements towards peace.
By then, many people will be gone forever.

She could not have known it then, but her words predicted the exact outcome of the war. Next month, November 1995, Bosnians, Croats, Serbs, and internationals meet in Dayton, Ohio, to hammer out a peace agreement. It comes too late to help the thousands at Srebrenica, killed and buried in mass graves—they are gone forever—those husbands, sons, fathers, grandfathers, uncles, and friends of the women and children I saw today in the refugee camps.

I return to Split to collect the suitcase with the dental supplies. I still feel stunned, as though I have understood nothing of this war. Or, maybe I understand too much.

The dental supplies weigh too much to take on the airlift to Sarajevo, so for three days I look for an overland ride. Finally, I find a convoy of eight semi-trailers hauling a shipment of flour. The supervisor agrees to let me ride along. I take a bus to Metković, about an hour away, and stay overnight in order to be ready for an early departure the next morning. The trip to Sarajevo is a grueling all-day drive through the mountains, with no comfort stops the whole day. At a stop along the road, I take refuge behind a wall in a destroyed house, as there are no other facilities, never considering until much later that the place could have been mined.

The staff at the children's dental clinic is delighted to receive the instruments and supplies. They ask if, when I return to the States, I can arrange to send them some dental journals as they are starved for the latest information. Before the siege, they used to receive American journals regularly.

By November, it is very cold in this part of the world. I often think of the women, children, and babies living in those plastic huts in Tuzla. But Sarajevo has its own desperate people. One morning, I ride the tram around the loop of the old town to the stop behind the Catholic cathedral. I am headed to the Music School a short block away. As we approach the stop, I feel a tug on my coat sleeve. I turn and face a stooped and frail old man dressed in a thin black raincoat. He hovers over a cloth sack on the floor near his feet. He mumbles a few words and I realize he wants me to carry the bag off the tram. I nod my head yes as the car comes to a jerky stop.

As I bend and grab the cloth handles, I am startled by the weight. Now I realize why he needs help. I can't imagine the content—maybe bricks. Once on the street, he reaches to reclaim his bag, but I don't give it up. I ask him where he is going and he motions toward the outdoor market about a block away. He walks close to me as we make our way on the crowded narrow sidewalk.

We enter the side aisle of the open-air market where those who cannot afford to rent a table squat beside their small treasures, until the police come and chase them away. He finds a niche and I lower the bag to the ground. He loosens the tie and one by one lifts out four two-liter plastic soda bottles filled with milk. In exchange for the few German marks he will earn today from the sale of the milk, he will buy some coffee, or sugar, or a bag of cabbage to pickle for winter, or a few pieces of firewood. My heart aches for this old man and the dozens of elderly like him who barely survive day to day. I say goodbye and pretend to leave, but walk around the corner and duck into a doorway. I pull my money belt from several layers of clothing and remove a fifty German mark note, money sent from supporters of the Sarajevo Project. I return to him and press it into his hand. As he realizes what it is, he looks at me in disbelief and begins to cry. I squeeze his hand, say goodbye, and hurry back down the street to the Music School.

In the afternoon, I visit a friend in the neighborhood to say good-bye. I carefully navigate the icy path through the courtyard connecting Renata's apartment building with the street one block over. As I pass through the arch to the street, I see an old woman rummaging through an overflowing garbage dumpster; she doesn't notice me. She wears a scarf on her head, several sweaters, but no coat. In lieu of boots, or shoes, she wears black rubber galoshes—standard humanitarian aid footwear for refugees.

She plucks a chunk of hard bread from the garbage, brushes it off, and carefully places it in her bag. I move closer and she realizes someone is watching her. She acknowledges my presence with a quick nod, but does not make eye contact. She returns to her task—find enough food to survive today.

I've never seen this woman before, yet I know her history. She is a refugee from Eastern Bosnia, maybe Foca, Srebrenica or Zepa. Bosnian Serbs systematically expelled her and many like her from their homes, and, as the Nazis did on the rail platforms at Auschwitz, the Serbs sent her in one direction, and her husband in another. She has not seen him since that day. Now she shares a room in a refugee collection center, with another old woman, with the same history. I cannot leave this woman without giving her the fifty German marks I have left. I walk over, greet the woman, and hand her the money. She handles the money as she did the bread—matter-of-factly, with little expression. She looks at it for a moment as if she is thinking; "Yes, this will help me survive." And she then stuffs it in her pocket. Tomorrow I leave Sarajevo. I am glad. I have nothing left to give.

I wake at 5:30 in the morning. Thirty minutes later I leave the apartment with my empty luggage and head toward the main street to hitchhike a ride to U.N. headquarters. As I turn the corner, I recognize two children from the Hotel Central Refugee Center. Fifty refugee children live in this battered former hotel. The center has priority for electricity, but there are no light bulbs in the halls or in the stairwells. On rainy days when the halls become a playground, the children play in the dark, reminding me of tiny cave creatures who have lived without light for so long they no longer need to see. The two children walking toward me are a boy about four, carrying a small cardboard box containing three loves of dirty bread, and his sister, about a year older. She wrestles a cardboard box twice her size—fuel for her mother's tiny tin stove. Light and warmth are hard to come by in this city. The children don't speak as they scurry in the direction of their one-room home in the Hotel Central. The children in the center are mostly from Eastern Bosnia and have lost their home, their father, probably grandfathers, and any other male relatives.

Yesterday, the initial signing of the Dayton Peace Agreement took place in Ohio. I looked for excitement and optimism in my friends here, but found none. They are disillusioned—too many ceasefires that didn't hold, too many safe havens not protected, too many friends and family killed on the streets of Sarajevo.

I leave Sarajevo not believing the war is really over. Some old problems will remain and new ones will arrive, but the guns surrounding Sarajevo for more than 1,200 days, creating the longest siege in modern history, will soon be gone. Even when the withdrawal is complete, the realization won't come to those living in Sarajevo for a long time. Like Pavlov's dogs, they will continue to walk faster through certain intersections and feel totally vulnerable when standing in full view of the mountains. Even after arriving safely in the United States, July Fourth fireworks send Renata and Irma into a clammy sweat. It is only when the guns fall silent that there is time to realize the true casualty count. No one has escaped unharmed or without loss.

I go to Sarajevo airport to take the airlift to Split in order to say goodbye to Renata. This is the last time I fly the airlift. Future trips offer local bus service from Split to Sarajevo in about six hours. I board the cargo plane along with one other passenger, a woman—reminiscent of my first trip with Anne Montgomery. We buckle ourselves in, but then one of the crew comes over and tells us to go to the cockpit. The captain asks us if we want to stand behind him and the co-pilot as the plane takes off. I think it is a bizarre idea and totally unsafe, but I can't resist his offer.

The acceleration down the runway and into the sky produces a rush of adrenaline reminding me of my first flight into Sarajevo. Instead of gasping at the view of charred houses, it is the free space, deep evergreen-covered mountains, and the red tile roofs below that take my breath away. In this moment, perhaps I should have said goodbye to Sarajevo, but I don't. I travel to Bosnia from the United States another five times, until I officially close the Sarajevo Project on July 13, 1998.

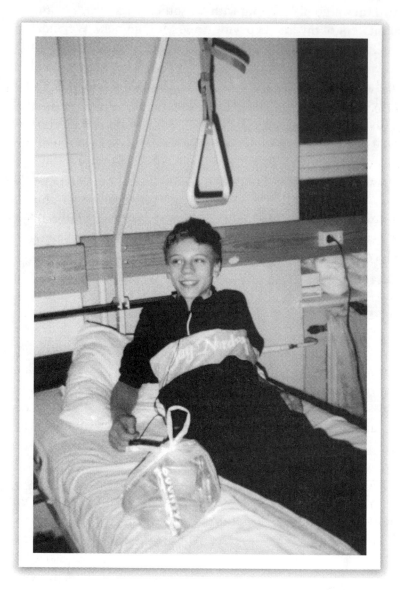

Mirza Alihodzić - Kosevo Hospital, September 1995

~ CHAPTER TWELVE ~
AFTER THE SIEGE—AN EPILOGUE

After the official signing of the Dayton Peace Agreement in Paris, on December 14, 1995, I return to Sarajevo five more times—as many times as I traveled there during the siege. In 1996, I visit in the spring and again in the fall, transporting supplies on behalf of the Sarajevo Project.

In May 1997, I return with my son, Matthew, and his friend Cody Doran. In our luggage, we carry dozens of plain colored T-shirts, textile paint, beads, colored markers, and other craft material for children's art projects. We also transport a cello packed among many pillows in a large cardboard box, and deliver it intact to the music school. Matt and Cody stay for one month, volunteering in a youth center situated on the former front line. When they arrive, a former trench, which ran right up to the front door of the center had only recently been filled.

Matt and Cody also spend time playing basketball with Mirza, the teenager I met in 1995, at the paraplegic clinic. Mirza lives at home now with his mother and sister. Thanks to an American donor, he has a new sports wheelchair, which allows him more mobility. As Matt and Cody and I walk around town, we notice workers cutting curbs to make wheelchair ramps, because of the great number of newly disabled.

Later in the summer, I rent a small apartment. Except for two brief trips back to Florida to collect supplies, I stay in Sarajevo until May 1998. During this time, I explore the possibility of transforming the Sarajevo Project into a permanent presence in Sarajevo, perhaps creating an after-school drop-in center for children. But clarity never comes, and after returning home in the summer of 1998, five years after first flying into Sarajevo, I close the project.

Each time I return to Sarajevo after the end of the siege I expect things to be better and superficially, they are. Many buildings are repaired, including the one in Renata's neighborhood where she almost lost her life in 1992. To look at the building now, a new-comer to the city would never suspect that on a clear spring day, a mortar explosion gutted it, dismembering several people who were drinking coffee in the courtyard. The day the building burned, the hot asphalt sidewalk softened, swallowing up thousands of bits of broken glass. Now, when the sun hits the asphalt, it glitters, a silent memorial to those who died there that day.

For several years after the siege ends, a small but telltale sign that war once occupied Sarajevo is the assortment of volunteer vegetable plants from the victory gardens that pop up each spring in yards and parks around the city. Each time I notice them, I re-member how desperate Sarajevans once were for salad and veg-etables.

The end of the war brought another type of peace on the streets. With the return of traffic lights and traffic police there is no more driving up on the sidewalk or speeding down the former Sniper Al-ley at 100 miles an hour.

Of course, the greatest consequence of the signing and imple-mentation of the Dayton Peace Agreement is the absence of shell-ing and sniper fire. At last, the aggressor's guns, which surrounded the city for more than three and a half years, are gone. Sarajevans know this, but they continue to walk faster through certain inter-sections. My intellect knows it too, but I doubt if I will ever be able to walk down the street in Sarajevo in full view of the mountains and not feel a little weak in the knees. Each time, my palms sweat and I feel a bit crazy. Was there a war, or was it only a nightmare? On five occasions, and for weeks at a time, from July 1993 to No-vember 1995, I lived a part of world history. Now, the memories seem distant and surreal.

With the weapons gone and free movement in and out of the city, residents are no longer forced to behave as rats, crawling out of Sarajevo through the tunnel. Public buses run between Sarajevo, Split, Tuzla, and Zagreb and throughout Bosnia. Beginning with my return in 1996, I no longer need U.N. identification to travel; the city is open.

In November 1999, I return to Sarajevo for several weeks to visit friends and collect material for this book, but not everyone wants to remember the war. I had hoped to interview a friend of Renata's, a doctor, who worked nearly round-the-clock throughout the war. When I call her, she says she is married, has a baby and doesn't want to think about the war. On a number of occasions during the war, on her rare day off, the three of us would sit together and drink Turkish coffee and half-seriously fanaticize how she might leave Sarajevo to attend some medical conference somewhere, just to have a brief relief from the war.

I call another woman, Azra, who lived in Renata's neighborhood. She is gracious as usual and invites me for Turkish coffee and cake. I ask if I can interview her for the book. Rather sarcastically, she says, "Why would you want to interview me? You were here in the war and saw everything. I'm a bit saturated with it all." Then she begins to cry. I feel terrible confronting her with the past and guilty because I remain privileged. Although I did risk my life by being in Sarajevo during the war, I did not live the siege in its entirety. I always had my escape valve, my U.N. press card. As long as the airport was open and the airlift operating, I came and left as I pleased. Though I shared some of Azra's war experiences, she is left with the full consequences of war. My life is intact, but she must pick up the pieces and attempt to rebuild hers.

Azra was in her final year of study at the university when the war began. She could not accept the fact that her education might end before she graduated. She said finishing her studies gave her a purpose in life and helped her survive.

Azra's university building was located in Bosnian Serb-held territory, so students and faculty could not go there. Azra quickly adds, "A university is more than a building, it is the professors." She often prepared for her exams by candlelight. When she did not have candles, she used cooking oil. She says, "It cost twenty dollars a liter, but I had to do it. In the war, I forgot everything material that once was important to me. I had to live in the moment, forgetting the past and the future. I thought then, when the war is over, I will live differently, not investing in a house or furniture. We Sarajevans experienced a special spirit in the war; now some of that spirit seems to have left. But, we have to go on with life. We have our everyday problems to solve but now we have time to think."

Azra did keep some of that special spirit. After she started working, she saved some money. She needed a car, but decided instead to go to Northern Europe on a holiday. She says, "Being under siege and cut off from the world scared me. I could not say, 'I've had enough of this, I am going.' Before the war, I always went somewhere several times a year, often to the seaside or mountains. I was never in this city four consecutive years without leaving. The siege was like a prison for me, but early in the war, sniper fire and shelling killed many people who were close to us. That's the worst of it. All the rest, the hunger and cold, it's just a child's game compared to the people we lost."

Like Azra, many others struggle to understand what happened in the war and how it changed them. Many parents thought they had shielded their children from the violence and impact of the war. But one mother discovered several years after the war ended, it was not possible. Ana and her husband bought their teenage son a large wallboard with colored pens, because he liked doing his math problems on a board. One day while he was at school, she went into his room. On the board she found a drawing of a bombed building with smoke rising from the roof. With the red marker, he had drawn people lying on the street in pools of blood. She said, "I realized then, he remembers everything. I tried to protect him from the war, but I can't erase the memories from his mind." Ana also struggles to understand how the war has changed her. She says, "Before 1992, we raised our kids to be kind, not to hit back. Now, we are still good people, but I teach my son not to be naïve, not to believe everything people say." She says, "In the war we were crazy! How could foreigners understand us? We were the only people in the world fighting to be together with those who were fighting not to be with us."

Since the war, when I meet children in Sarajevo, I mentally calculate what age they might have been during the siege. Next, I wonder what the war stole from them—a parent, sibling, grandparent, friend, their physical or mental health, a home, or the sense of well being and safety every child deserves. I know for sure, the war took something.

When I first visited Sarajevo in the summer of 1993, I saw gutted buildings and thousands of wooden markers on fresh graves. In Kosevo hospital I saw a ten-year-old missing a foot because a Serb sniper had deliberately targeted her. I saw a toddler with his tiny body swollen, riddled with shrapnel wounds and struggling to breathe because there was no electricity to run the respirator. I thought then: "This is the horror of war." But as I continue my connection, my journey with Sarajevo, I realize the consequences of war reach far beyond the period of actual fighting. For everyone who lived in Sarajevo during the siege, time is divided into two parts—before the siege and after the siege.

From afar, or in the history books, war often looks like one large violent event or, sometimes, many smaller battles. As a witness, I learned war is made up of a million small, ordinary and extraordinary moments lived every day under the most uncomfortable and life-threatening circumstances.

War is hunger and thirst. It is feeling helpless to protect your children. It is giving birth in a hospital without electricity or water, and washing diapers in a freezing river under the cover of darkness. It is losing a relative or friend to a sniper's bullet, or mortar explosion, or from natural causes, and having to bury them at night because during the day snipers target funerals. War is a fourteen-year-old boy shot by a sniper and permanently forced into a wheelchair.

War is feeling abandoned because the international community refuses to act on the side of justice. War is receiving food or medicine years beyond its expiration date. War is living in a damp basement. It is longing for a hot shower. War is a hungry man who has no cooking facilities. While helping unload food aid, he is invited to take some candy bars. His hands tremble as he surrenders his pride and desperately stuffs as many bars as he can into his pockets.

War is celebrating birthdays, weddings, and anniversaries. It is making war cake with improvised ingredients. War is deciding to have a baby. War is divorce. War is planning an escape through the tunnel. It is deciding to stay. War is an old woman who commits suicide by jumping from her kitchen balcony. War is defying the enemy by refusing to despair. War is a new bar of soap. It is coffee with sugar. It is playing the piano, dancing, laughing, working, and studying. War is growing tomatoes and onions in a rooftop garden or on the windowsill. War is a community oven. It is a war school in your living room. War is a letter received from friends or family outside of Bosnia, or a letter sent from Sarajevo, carried by a journalist or other international person. War is a day or night without shelling.

War is genocide—thousands of persons forced from their homes and thousands more killed and dumped into mass graves. War is an old woman who watches helplessly as the aggressor beats and kills her husband of fifty years. War is Bosnians scattered to the four corners of the globe. Like a raging river, war uproots and transports people to where they never expected or wanted to be.

As the Bosnians I met in the siege piece the puzzle of their lives back together, sometimes parts are missing, creating gaping holes, but they fill those places with their sheer determination to move forward and overcome their suffering.

Irma was still a child when I first met her in 1994. She used to tell me then, "I want to go away to some little island and live my little, little life in peace. I don't think that is asking too much." Often now, she remembers the song she listened to that day she left her house and her childhood behind: *Who knows, maybe there is another world waiting for me? ...Who knows, maybe one in a thousand, one of the luckiest I will be.* Irma says, "I feel blessed I survived the war along with my parents and sisters. Now, my war experience influences the way I look at the world and the way I make everyday relationships. I define myself as a successful and ambitious person in my struggle to survive living far away from home, and in having to encounter cultural differences everyday. I will never know what I could have been if war hadn't destroyed years of my life, but I am alive and have been given a chance, and that is all that matters; the rest is up to me." Irma is married and attends college full time. She lives in the same town as her sister Selma.

Selma is also married and has a baby. I proudly attended her college graduation several years ago. Selma and Irma's parents and little sister returned to Bosnia to live in the house they once lost. The aggressor lived in their house until the end of the war, and when they left, stripped it of everything, including the sink, toilet, bathtub, electrical fixtures, and even the floorboards. Slowly, Irma's parents have repaired their house, but they can never repair their memory of the fear they felt the day they were expelled from their home and neighborhood, warned never to return.

Renata lives in Florida. After the war, her husband joined her in the United States, but soon they separated and divorced. She remarried and has a second child, a girl. For more than eight years various jobs paid the rent, but she always yearned to bring dance into her life again. Recently, she opened her own ballet school. On the walls hang three photographs—all pictures of stately wooden doors. The first is the ballet school in Pancevo, Serbia, where she began her ballet career at age five, after begging her parents for lessons. The second is the music school in Sarajevo, where she continued her ballet studies and graduated high school. And the third is the National Theater in Sarajevo, where her professional ballet career began only to be cut short by the war. Now, Renata has entered through another door, that of her new ballet studio in Tampa. The door is made of metal and glass, the kind typically found in American strip malls. The door is definitely not as impressive as the other three, but, nonetheless, it is a portal, an entry to reclaim a love that war tried to steal from her.

Alma married an Australian who was working in Sarajevo. They had a baby and left Sarajevo to live in Australia. Alma's mother died soon after the war ended.

Farida Musanović continues to work as a piano teacher in the Secondary Music School in Sarajevo. Since the years of the siege, she has been active in the international project *Women for Women*.

Ana lives in Sarajevo with her husband and son. Soon after the war, she applied for a job and was told she was too old, although she was only in her mid-thirties. She says, "I was too old because war stole almost four years of my life. Now, when people ask my age, I subtract the war years."

Azra received her university degree, and lives and works in Sarajevo.

Mirza still lives in Sarajevo with his mother and sister. After high school, he wanted to enroll in the Faculty of Physical Culture/Sports Faculty, but says the Ministry of Education doesn't provide a curriculum for disabled people. He then tried to find work, but public transportation and many buildings are not accessible to the disabled. In spite of these disappointments, Mirza is optimistic. He says, "My life is difficult, but I am ready to fight for a better future. I have a strong will and wish to live and attain something in my life. I hope my life will be better one day."

In 1993, before I went to Sarajevo, and almost a year before I met her, fourteen-year-old Irma wrote to an unknown pen pal: " … if you want to know the truth about my brave people, come here and judge for yourself this unjust war." Unknowingly, I accepted Irma's invitation and went to Bosnia to see for myself. As Irma perceived the reality of the war and her people, I found the same to be true—the war unjust and the people brave.

Webster's Dictionary defines the word *witness* as: *attestation of a fact or event; one that gives evidence; one who testifies in a cause; or one who has personal knowledge of something*. When I began this journey, I did not realize being a witness to this historic event made me part of it and carried with it the never-ending responsibility of being a voice for those in the siege who had none. I now testify through my personal experience, the crime of the siege of Sarajevo did occur and ordinary citizens there, through fully living the routine of their daily lives, rose above horrendous obstacles not only to survive, but to also retain their dignity and humanity. The images of Sarajevo under siege remain forever imbedded in my soul.

Left: Matthew Beekman
Center: Mirza Alihodzić
Right: Cody Doran
Photo: Linda Beekman

Left: Linda Beekman
Right: Mirza Alihodzić
Photo: Jerry Bilton

~ Appendix ~

The Sarajevo Project

Soon after coming home from my first visit to Sarajevo in September 1993, I organized the Sarajevo Project in order to collect funds and supplies to return to the besieged city in February 1994. The Tampa Bay Peace Education Program, a project of the St. Petersburg Friends Meeting (Quakers), accepted the project under its sponsorship. Two years later, I asked the St. Petersburg Friends Meeting to take the Sarajevo Project directly under its care.

What began in the fall of 1993 as an effort to raise enough supplies and funds for one trip mushroomed into providing for nine trips between 1994 and 1998. During these years, the Sarajevo Project provided more than a ton of supplies for Bosnia valued at $40,000. During the siege alone, I shuttled more than a thousand pounds of aid in my backpack and luggage. The Sarajevo Project also provided more than $15,000 in small grants to individuals and groups.

On each trip, my goals were always the same.

Be a witness for peace—a voice for those who had none.

Facilitate communication between those in Sarajevo and their friends and families in other parts of the world.

Take as much aid as possible.

Although I founded, organized and facilitated the project, from its inception it quickly took on a life of its own. Many people of various ages, religions, political beliefs and economic and ethnic backgrounds joined to help Bosnia through the project. To all who sustained, fostered, encouraged and cared for the Sarajevo Project (and sometimes cared for me), thank you! Together we accomplished what none of us could have done alone.

I am deeply grateful to the Tampa Bay Peace Education Program for helping get the project started and to the St. Petersburg Friends Meeting for your spiritual and material considerations. The Sarajevo Project could not have existed without your help.

Also, a special thanks to Karen Putney, who served as project coordinator in 1997-98, while I was in Bosnia, and to those who at various times, served on the Sarajevo Project Steering Committee

Many thanks to Susan Sontag for endorsing my work in Bosnia in the Sarajevo Project brochure, and to Yoko Ono, and Pete and Toshi Seeger for generously contributing to the project.

It is not possible to list all the donors to the Sarajevo Project, but you all made a difference and I am grateful for your support. The following individuals, companies, organizations and churches gave exceptional help. Thank you to:

Bob and Janet Aldridge, Pam Arnold, Glenn Atkins, Hope Bastian, Jerry Bilton, Caroline Bloodworth, Patrice Callaghan, James R. Carlson, Ilise Cohen, Martha Collins, Edward Cozak, Edith Daly, Gail Daneker, Eva Del Cid, Patricia Ditto, Shawna Doran, Carol Tanner Dotterer, Jim & Shelley Douglass, Debra Doyle, Carol Drewnowski, Mary Fentress, Hetty Friedman, Garry Fullerton, Dorothy Gates, Annette Godow, Rena-paulette Guay, Judy Geary, Joan Given, Maj. Robert Goulka, Beverly Grossman, Herb & Pam Haigh, Lynn Carol Henderson, Peter F. Hornik, Donald Irish, Brent Jordan, Elaine Jordan, Chris & Debra Kelly, Ken Kinzel, Judith Laddon, Len Leeb, John Levin, Tedford & Margaret Lewis, Wendy Loomas, Marlin Eric McAfee, Ralph & Pat McLaury, Anne Miller, Irene Miller, Harvey Mirsky, Joel Mitnick, Farida Musanović, Marie Nelson, Inge Nickerson, Christine O'Brien, Meta Osborn, Ruth Hyde Paine, Martha Pihaylic, Adam Pinsker, The Putney Family, Jan Reiner, Margaret Rigg, Ron Anton Rocz, Roy E. Runkle, Gretel Von Pichke, Jacquin Sanders, William Sax, Nancy Schaub, Joan Schell, Marjorie Sibley, Suzie Siegel, Kim Smieja, The Rev. John R. Smucker III, Roberta Spivek, John & Sheila Stewart, Barbara Thompson, Rifat Uzunović, The Rev. Donald Wagner, Suzanne Wicks, David and Jean Alexander Williams, Barbara Wolfe, Capt. Lisa Woodbury, Linda & Gordon Woodcock, Cecilia Yocum, and Eileen Zingaro.

Abbott Pharmaceutical/Ross Products, C.R. Bard Inc., Ballet Etc./Kathy Loscher, Capezio/Ballet Makers, Dana Undies, Danskin Inc., Fellowship Magazine/Richard L. Deats, Freed of London LTD., Gene's Upholstery & Vinyl Repair, Kerr Corp., GFWC Clearwater Junior Woman's Club, K.I.D.S. Association, Gaynor Minden Inc., Mirella Dancewear, Prima Soft/Marlena Juniman, Osceola High School, Joseph H. & Frieda K. Ross Trust, St. Petersburg Times, Shar Products Co., Star Styled Mfg./Philip Giberson, Tampa Tribune, Turtle Bay Music School, USF Dance Dept./Gretchen Warren, WMNF Community Radio, William Carter Co., Womyn's Energy Bank, and Yamaha Corp. of America.

Athens Friends Meeting, Georgia; Atlanta Friends Meeting; Baton Rouge Friends Meeting; Boone Friends Meeting, North Carolina; Cambridge Friends, Massachusetts; Carawba Valley Friends, North Carolina; Charleston Friends Meeting; Clearwater Friends Meeting, Florida; Decorah Friends Meeting, Idaho; Eastern Hills Friends, Ohio; Friends Meeting of Fort Myers, Florida; Greenville Friends Meeting, South Carolina; Good Shepherd Catholic Church, Huntsville, Alabama; Honolulu Friends; Lake Region Unitarian Universalist Fellowship, Florida; Langley Hill Friends Meeting, Washington D.C.; Lubbock Friends Meeting, Texas; Mattapoisett Friends Meeting, Massachusetts; Midcoast Monthly Meeting (First Day School), Maine; New Orleans Friends Meeting; Oshkosh Monthly Meeting, Wisconsin; Palo Alto Monthly Meeting of Friends, California; Plainfield Friends Church, North Carolina; Quaker Life/Friends United Meeting, Indiana; Reston Friends Meeting, Virginia; St. Louis Friends Meeting; St. Paul United Church of Christ, Lebanon, Illinois; Salem Upper Springfield Monthly Meeting, Ohio; San Jose Friends Meeting; Tallahassee Friends Meeting, Florida; Tampa Friends Meeting; Twin City Friends Meeting, Minnesota; Unitarian Universalist Church, Clearwater, Florida; West Palm Beach Meeting, Florida; and Woodstown Monthly Meeting, New Jersey.

Finally, thank you to my family, who put up with my travels for five years: my son, Matthew; his father, Frank Beekman Jr.; my sisters, Nancy Lopatin and Janis Mockler; and my father, David Flynn. My mother, Dorothy Flynn, died in April 1997. From the beginning, she wasn't thrilled about me leaving her grandson and going to a war zone. She said she would not help with the project but would lend support to Matthew while I was away. But in 1996, I found her helping me sort a thousand fundraiser letters by ZIP code. Later that year in her living room, we matched 3,000 pair of children's snap pajamas according to color and size. Her help meant a lot to me.

The following summarizes some of the aid the Sarajevo Project provided.

February 1994: Three weeks in Sarajevo. Delivered baby food, baby clothes, diapers, first aid supplies, dried fruit and nuts, vitamins, sweaters, socks, underwear, candles, flashlight, batteries. $1,000 used for food and small grants given to various individuals. Delivered money and food to four individuals from their Bosnian relatives in the United States and in England. Delivered pen pal letters from students at Osceola High School in Florida. On two side trips to Italy, mailed letters and made phone calls for people in Sarajevo to relatives and friends in other counties.

October 1994: Three weeks in Sarajevo. Ballet supplies valued at more than $4,000 donated to Sarajevo Ballet Co. Two side trips to Italy to buy food for people in Renata's neighborhood and Irma's family: coffee, cheese, soup mix, sausage, instant potatoes, spices, dried tomatoes, tea, dried fruit, bulb for flashlight, bicycle tire repair kit, butter, jam, juice powder, Nescafe, saccharine, honey, pens, chocolate. $1,000 in funds provided.

March 1995: Two weeks in Sarajevo. Focus of trip was children at the Mjedenica School. From United States brought underwear, socks, mittens, T-shirts, crayons, markers, watercolors, hair ribbons, barrettes, combs, handkerchiefs, vitamins, baseball caps, Lego sets, pencils, chocolate, first aid supplies, toothbrushes, soap, sewing supplies. Food purchased for school: 100 kilos potatoes, 20 kilos bananas, 12 kilos onions, 20 kilos oranges, 4 kilos garlic, 7 kilos cheese, 3 kilos sausage, 20 kilos tangerines. Food and funds also donated to various individuals. In total, $1,000 provided.

September 1995: Three months in Sarajevo, Tuzla and Split.

Attended Helsinki Citizens Assembly Conference in Tuzla. $300 given to refugees and other people in Tuzla. Delivered money from Renata's father to his elderly mother in Tuzla. $1,500 given to Renata, now a refugee in Split. Delivered dental supplies to children's dental clinic in Sarajevo, musical instruments and music notation books to music school. Food and other supplies donated to several gypsy families. Catheters donated to paraplegic clinic in Sarajevo. Food, clothes and book donated to Mirza, fourteen-year-old boy shot by sniper. $1,700 donated to individuals in Sarajevo.

March 1996: 10 days in Sarajevo. $1,000 given in $20 grants to fifty children at the Bjelave refugee collection center in Sarajevo. Sarajevo Project provides funds for Saturday ballet classes at same center. Drum, ballet shoes and clarinet donated to music school. $1,000 given in small, equal grants to teachers of the Secondary Music School who worked there during the entire war. Donated large shipment of baby items to project in Tuzla.

October 1996: Three months in Tuzla with several weekends in Sarajevo. $15,000 shipment of children's sleepers and snap-pajamas donated to project in Tuzla. Three violins, two trumpets, two clarinets donated to music school in Sarajevo. $1,000 donated to Secondary Music School to refurbish music library. Shipment of ballet supplies sent to primary music school. Underwear and toys to Bjelave Orphanage. $1,000 donated to various refugees and people in need. $600 electronic piano tuning instrument donated to Secondary Music School (transported from United States by staff of United Methodist Committee on Relief). $576 delivered to Bjelave Orphanage, donated by three groups in San Jose, Calif.

May 1997: Five months in Sarajevo. Organize visit of Cody Doran and my son, Matthew Beekman, who spend one month volunteering at a Catholic Relief Service youth club. Through the help of American military in Sarajevo, before I leave the States I ship more than 500 pounds of arts and crafts supplies and several hundred children's books for English classes at the youth club. Delivered fine art supplies to art high school in Sarajevo. $2,000 given to refugees in Tuzla and Sarajevo. Violin and clarinet donated to music school in Tuzla. $300 donated to Law School in Sarajevo for books. Supplies given to Be My Friend project in Sarajevo. Cello brought from United States delivered to primary music school, Sarajevo. $500 donated to various individuals.

October 1997: $1,000 given to refugees and other people in need. Christmas and other supplies delivered to CRS Youth Club, Be My Friend and World Vision projects.

February-May 1998: Final months in Sarajevo on behalf of Sarajevo Project. $1,000 grant received from Jewish organization distributed through the help of the Women to Women project to victims of ethnic cleansing. Music and dance supplies donated to both music schools. Work with Francesca Sola, a ballet dancer from Belgium, in procuring local aid in Sarajevo for a group of refugees living in an abandoned building. $2,000 donated to refugees and to students for educational needs.

July 1998: The Sarajevo Project closes.

Faceless Refugee
Youth Club-Sarajevo 1997

Plaster Masks
Youth Club-Sarajevo 1997

~ READING AND WEB SITE RESOURCES ~

- *The Black Book of Bosnia,* by the Editors of the New Republic, Basic Books, 1996.
- *Bosnia: A Short History,* by Malcom Noel, New York University Press, 1996.
- *The Bridge Betrayed (Religion and Genocide in Bosnia-Herzegovina),* by Michael Sells, California University Press, 1998.
- *The Bridge over the Drina,* by Ivo Andric, University of Chicago Press, 1984.
- *End Game, The Betrayal and Fall of Srebrenica,* by David Rohde, Westview Press, 1998.
- *Fax from Sarajevo, A Story of Survival,* by Joe Kubert, Dark Horse Comics, 1996.
- *Genocide in Bosnia,* by Norman Cigar, Texas A&M University Press, 1995.
- *Harvest in the Snow, My Crusade to Rescue the Lost Children of Bosnia,* by Ellen Blackman, Brassey's, 1997.
- *Letters from Sarajevo, Voices from a Besieged City,* by Anna Cataldi (Editor), Harper Collins, 1994.
- *Love Thy Neighbor: A Story of War,* by Peter Maas, Alfred A. Knopf, 1996.
- *Mass Rape, The War Against Women in Bosnia-Herzegovina,* by Alexandra Stiglmayer (Editor), University of Nebraska Press, 1995.
- *My People, A Story of the Jews,* by Abba Eban, Random House, 1984.
- *Sarajevo Daily, A City and Its Newspaper Under Siege,* by Tom Gjelten, Harper Collins, 1995.
- *Sarajevo, A Portrait of the Siege,* by Matthew Naythons (Producer), Warner Books, 1994.
- *Slaughterhouse: Bosnia and the Failure of the West,* by David Rieff, Simon and Schuster, 1995.
- *Witness to Genocide,* by Roy Gutman, Macmillan, 1993.

- *Yugoslavia: Death of a Nation,* by Laura Silber and Allan Little, Penguin Books, 1996.
- *Zlata's Diary, A Child's Life in Sarajevo,* by Zlata Filpović, Penguin Books, 1994.

- www.bosnia.org.uk
- www.cco.caltech.edu/~bosnia
- www.friendsofbosnia.org
- www.un.org/icty
- www.warcake.com